LISTEN TO THE CARDS

I0461363

AN INTUITIVE DAILY TAROT JOURNAL

EX LIBRIS: _____

YEAR: _____

DECK USED: _____

PAPERBACK: ISBN 979-8-9865062-0-3
LISTEN TO THE CARDS: AN INTUITIVE TAROT JOURNAL
PUBLISHED BY HAVEN COTTAGE PRESS
ANGLETON, TEXAS

Thank you so very much

For your purchase of Listen to the Cards: An Intuitive Daily Tarot Journal. Tarot can be a sacred spiritual practice as well as a tool for mindfulness and self-awareness. I designed this journal for anyone who wants to develop their intuitive card reading skills. As a full time teacher who studies many forms of divination, I am often asked how to get started reading tarot. By setting up the steps in an easy to follow workbook form, both novice and seasoned readers alike can develop their intuitive skills with daily intention. My goal was to deliver the goods in a quick and dirty way so you can spend your time actually developing your intuition rather than just reading about it. Listen to the cards is a 365 day journal that gives the tarot practitioner a intentional course of study in an easy to use format. You will learn by doing, and at the end of this year you will be reading tarot intuitively with confidence!

Warmest Regards,

Jacquelyn

Whether you're a complete newbie, or someone that wants to be more intentional about tarot, I've assembled the need-to-know information that will give you a solid foundation in your practice. CHECK OUT THE USER GUIDE

RESOURCES INCLUDE: Card Care and Feeding, Reading the Cards, Reading by the Moon, Major Arcana keyword and signifier tables, Minor Arcana symbolism/numerology and keyword tables, Birth Card Exercise, Key Card Indicators, Tarot Tips and Tricks, Tarot Question Stems, 12 Tarot spreads, Deck Dedication, Grounding Exercise, Intuition Exercises, Tarot Meditation, Intuition Prompts, and The "Me" Page: a self-love exercise.

JOURNAL FEATURES have you covered for another journey around the sun:
Yearly Outlook card spread with Yearly Intention Exercise
Monthly Calendar with open dating
Monthly 6 card spread
Monthly New Moon Spread and Intention Exercise
Monthly Full Moon Spread and Intention Exercise
Weekly single card draw with intention/affirmation
Daily 3 card draws with reflection
Note pages

MONTH:___January_____ FULL MOON: __cancer_____ NEW MOON:__capricorn___

Sunday	Monday	Tuesday	Wednesday	Thursday	Friday	Saturday
						1 Smudge Day
2 New Moon	**3**				**7**	**8** coffee with Mom
9 Movies with cody and Sloan	**10**			**14** car service 4 p.m.		**15**
16	**17** Full Moon campfire night	**18**	**19**	**20**	**21**	**22** Austin trip to see Molly →
23 →	**24**	**25** Dentist 2:30	**26**	**27** Pickup grocery order 4:00	**28** Hang out with Nessa	**29**
30	**31**					

Check out the user guides on the next few pages:

Personalize your journal. Color, draw, fill in the blanks, make notes and make it you own!

January

DECK USED: _Arthurian Legend_____

9 of Pentacles Reversed
MONTHLY ENERGY

Page of wands Reversed	8 of Swords	King of Swords Reversed	..e Magician	Ace of Swords
LOVE	MONEY	WORK	HEALTH	SPIRIT

WHAT ARE ASTROLOGICAL HAPPENINGS THIS MONTH?

WRITE OR DRAW YOUR CARD MEANINGS!

MONTHLY ENERG...: ...n self-worth this month. Am I doing enough to support my growth? You are a hard worker. Do... ...yourself. Be careful not to over-invest in work? I don't think people should spend their whol... ...ng. Watch out for shallow people.

LOVE: consider whether I'm well su... ...to commitment. Indecision and lack of communication seem to be a problem. Stirrings of something new, redirect energy into self-love.

MONEY: May feel bound and trapped by previous decisons, inability to free yourself from a difficult situation at this time. Personal effort and courage is needed. Stay strong. This too shall pass.

WORK: You are good at your job. You contribute talents to society. Harmony in your environment (now that I'm used to it). sensitive to unseen forces.

HEALTH: Manifestation: focus and get what you want. use resourcefulness, inspired action. How can I grow this month?

PLENTY OF SPACE TO MAKE NOTES ON YOUR INTERPRETATIONS

SPIRIT: could experience a breakthrough. I'm feeling flooded with new ... ...ill be improved. Be open to messages.

END OF THE MONTH REFLECTION: I feel like I'm growing at work. Both my team and my students seem happy. Things are definitely changing, but this time feels very heavy. Financial stress feels right on with this reading. I'd like to spen... get on a better schedule.

THE WAXING CRESCENT MOON PHASE IS AN IDEAL TIME FOR REFLECTION. WHEN THIS MOON PHASE ALIGNS WITH MONTH'S END, YOUR ABILITY TO REFLECT WILL BE AMPLIFIED, AND THE DEPTH OF YOUR REFLECTIONS WILL BE POWERFUL

nd the house and

Queen of cups	**Week of:** ___August 23-29___
	INTENTION: ___I will be pres~~...~~ ages I am meant to receive.___
	AFFIRMATION: ___I will tre~~...~~ and love I deserve.___

A PLACE FOR AFFIRMATION AND INTENTIONS

INTERPRETATION: ___Be compassionate, caring, and kind. Lean into your emotional side this week.___ ___Exhibit patience and understanding for others. Trust your intuition.___

REFLECTION: ___A tough week for many of my people. Lots accomplished that I needed to get done.___

DECK USED: Deck of the Bastard

WEEKLY SINGLE CARD DRAW SECTION

Monday the 23rd

Knight of Pentacles	1. ___Methodical person. Patience to accomplish tasks. Hard work will lead to___ ___Trustworthy, reliable person.___
Knight of Swords	2. ___Powerful figure. Balance of compassion and responsibility. Moves forward with___ ___determination. No stopping energy of new project.___
	3. ___Possible turn of bad luck. resistant to something? Is this a negative cycle being broken.___
Wheel of fortune reversed	REFLECTION: ___Today required problem solving skills, but we ended in success.___
	DECK USED: Arthurian Legend

Tuesday the 24th

8 of wands	1. ___High level of energy and progress. Don't resist. Focus on the actions you want to take.___
10 of coins	2. ___Accomplishment, completion, financial abundance, commitment to future and family.___

DAILY 3 CARD DRAW. WHAT DOES MY DAY LOOK LIKE?

	3. ___Love between 2 people, commitment and partnership with h~~...~~___
2 of cups	REFLECTION: ___In the weeds at work, but growth with new friendship___
	DECK USED: Deck of the Bastard

Wednesday the 25th

Page of pentacles	1. ___New beginnings, project? Able to manifest dreams and goals, motivation and energy to begin___
4 of swords reversed	2. ___In danger of burnout. Rest and relax. Need to introvert in order to rest and focus so you___ ___can tackle goals with renewed vigor.___
	3. ___Creative energy is flowing. Open yourself up to new things. Trust your intuition.___
Page of cups	REFLECTION: ___Taking on too much at work. Going to have some me time this evening___
	DECK USED: Mary-El Tarot

Thursday the 26th

1. creativity may be blocked. Prioritize self care. Get back to nature. what inspires you?

2. check your connection to power. Are you ma_____ ego or soul? Does this represent me or someone around me?

3. Disharmony in relationships or h_____ than usual. This could also be internal self-love is needed.

REFLECTION: Introspective too___ need me time.

DECK USED: crow tarot

[handwritten note overlay:] OPEN DATING! IF YOU MISS SOME TIME YOU CAN STILL USE YOUR WEEKLY PAGES.

Empress reversed
Emperor reversed
Lovers reversed

Friday the 27th

1. Working for what you want. Time now equals success down the road

2. Nostalgia, happy memories, living in the past? Harmony. Seek inner child and let her be my teacher.

3. Mental clarity. Plain spoken, maturity, trut___ ___lent woman unafraid to speak truthfully.

REFLECTION: Today called on ___ ___nd communication skills.

DECK USED: Rider-waite

[handwritten note overlay:] I DOUBLE DOG DARE YOU TO STOP AT ONE DECK!

7 of pentacles
6 of cups
Queen of swords

Saturday the 28th

1. caught in a difficult decision. Lacking information. Use intuition. Stalemate, caught in the middle.

2. Things haven't turned out as planned. Get over it and get out of the past. Forgiveness will free you. Prepare for new opportunities.

3. Future planning, progress, and maximizing potential. Travel opportunity. Big things are on the horizon.

REFLECTION: Difficult conversation with co-worker

DECK USED: cat's Eye Tarot

[handwritten note overlay:] DRAW A PICTURE OF YOUR CARDS: USE SYMBOLS

2 of swords reversed
5 of cups
3 of wands

Sunday the ___

1. Renewed hope and faith. Blessings from the universe, find your sense of purpose, generosity.

2. Listen to your heart. It's time to decide to stay or go. Are you happy where you are or is it time to seek something else?

3. Happiness, joy, and emotional contentment. Family. Positive commitments.

REFLECTION: I need to push through the difficulties, because the reward is far greater.

DECK USED: Deck of the Bastard

The Star
8 of cups reversed
10 of cups

Card Care and Feeding

Tradition suggests that a tarot deck should be received as a gift from a loved one as it will carry that energy with it. It is also believed that a novice reader should receive their first deck from their mentor/teacher. I like to keep these traditions alive, but I acknowledge it is perfectly acceptable to buy your own deck, and I would even say it is advantageous to let it choose you.

STORE YOUR CARDS in a silk scarf, luxurious fabric, velvet pouch, or wooden box where they are protected. I keep whatever crystals speak to me with my decks.

CARD CLEANSING/CHARGING can be done through (Earth) salt burial or crystal cleansing, (Air) shuffle and reordering the deck or sound cleansing, (Fire) Smudging/Incense, (Water) moon energy, and (Spirit) visualization. Whatever feels right to you is always the right answer.

CLEANSE YOUR CARDS WHEN they have been touched by another person, they fall on the floor, you have received them second hand, you've had a particularly draining reading, your cards have been sitting unused for some time, they have been exposed to negative energy, you feel disconnected from them, or readings are lacking clarity.

BOND WITH YOUR CARDS like you would a friend. The deeper the bond to your cards, the more clarity they will give you. Introduce yourself. spend time with them, converse with them. Carry them on your person if you can. Sleep with them in your pillowcase. Ask permission before altering your deck in any way. Interview them and let them tell you about themself.

BLESSING OR CONSECRATING YOUR DECK
Tarot cards are sacred tools that act as your conduit to Spirit. We want them to guide us, provide clarity, and protection. Dedicating your deck to a sacred purpose tunes them into a higher vibrational frequency and deepens your connection.

GROUNDING is a practice that brings balance to mind, body, and soul. It means centering yourself and connecting to your spirit. Nature always offers the best ways to ground. Find the element that calls to you and connect with it. Breathe and focus through your grounding exercise.

MEDITATING with an individual card can open your intuition to deeper meanings. As with any meditation you want to choose the right environment. Follow the 4 steps to reading intuitively. Breathe, relax, focus, journal your thoughts afterward, and reflect.

Reading the Cards

The skill you want to develop for tarot is your intuition. Intuition takes tarot beyond memorization. Learning the traditional meanings of the tarot deck comes with time, study, and practice, but you will gain personal insight as well. The more layers of meaning you add, the more depth your readings will have.

4 Steps to Reading Intuitively
1. Speak what you see on the card. Obvious and literal interpretation/imagery.
2. Look for symbols. Use your own experiences and intuition to give the symbols meaning. Remember that these are *YOUR* cards. Let them talk to you.
3. Apply these meanings to the question that is being asked and listen to your cards.
4. As you connect these messages, be open to your cards and what they want to tell you.

3 Steps to Reading Reversals
1. Look at the opposite meaning. If the upright card suggests chaos then it's opposite could suggest stability or structure.
2. Look at it as decreased in strength. The inverted card can also signify the same meaning, but with less potency. A card signifying harmony would still be true, but in a lesser measure.
3. Look at it as internal vs. external. Upright cards are representing what is going on in the situation, externally. A reversal can be interpreted as what is going on internally.

Shuffling and cutting
Whatever feels right to you is always the right answer. Here are a few shuffling options:
- Pile your deck face down, mix up the cards using both hands, and regather your cards.
- Hold the deck in your dominant hand and feed smaller sections into your other hand, alternating each section on top/or underneath.
- Riffle and bridge- casino style card shuffling that takes some practice.

Once shuffled, cards can be pulled from the top or bottom of a deck. They can also be fanned out for selection. Cutting the deck is another option open to you. You can opt to have a querent cut the deck into smaller stacks from which you pull their cards.

The Phases of the Moon

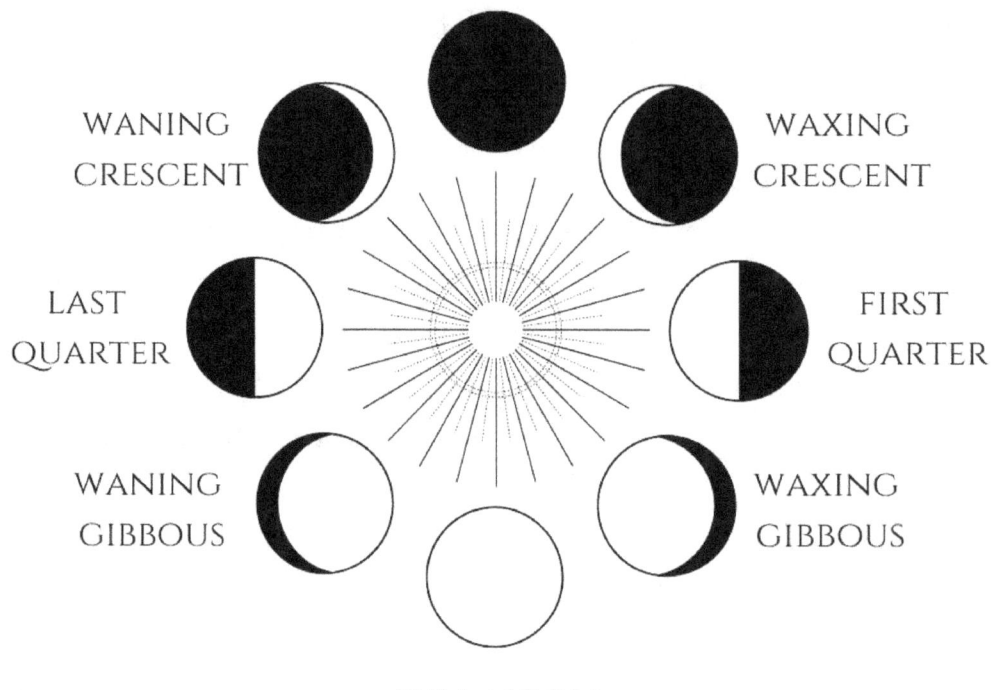

WORKING WITH THE MOON CONNECTS US TO THE NATURAL FLOW OF LIFE. AS THE MOON GROWS SO SHOULD OUR ACTIONS FOLLOWING OUR INTENTIONS.

NEW MOON- Dream and set intentions. What do you want to accomplish?

WAXING CRESCENT Plan and prepare practical steps towards your goals.

FIRST QUARTER Commit and take action, solve problems, and make tough decisions.

WAXING GIBBOUS Refine your plan and shift direction as needed.

FULL MOON Enjoy illumination and celebrating how far you've come toward your intention.

WANING GIBBOUS Accept the benefits of your actions and be grateful.

LAST QUARTER Release what no longer serves you and reconnect with Spirit.

WANING CRESCENT Reflect and rest, practice self-care, and seek spiritual nourishment.

Reading by the Moon

ALWAYS TRUST YOUR INTUITION. If it feels right, then it probably is. The same is true when reading tarot. There are times when messages come in clearer than other times, but your practice is determined by you and there are many factors that can influence the clarity of a reading. Traditionally, the most clear and precise readings happen on Samhain (October 31-November 1) and Beltane (May 1) because the veil is thinnest.

Reading Under a New Moon

New Moon energy is showing potential. Cards will give honesty, but may lack clarity. For important readings it might be best to wait until the moon can illuminate the path.

Reading Under a Waxing Moon

Waxing moon energy is about rebirth and increase. This is an ideal time to ask the cards about beginnings, new projects or challenges. The answers will show you where and how to move forward.

Reading Under a Full Moon

Full moon energy is powerful illumination. A reader's intuition and wisdom are enhanced. The cards give the most clear answers during the full moon phase.

Reading Under the Waning Moon

Waning moon energy is about shedding, clearing, letting go. This is an ideal time to ask the cards about purging and endings. The answers will show you where and how to tie up loose ends.

READING FOR YOURSELF can be trickier than reading for someone else because we tend to get intuition and expectation mixed up together and we don't always walk away with clear answers. Grounding yourself is essential. Keep an open mind and let go of the expectation of what you want to see. Take your time. Reflect on the traditional meaning of the cards to avoid mistaking expectation for intuition. There is no shame in going back to definitions when it comes to reading for yourself. Journal and reflect. Sometimes messages only make sense after reflection.

My favorite way to read for myself is to ask a single question, but use 3 cards to answer it. I find that I get readings with lots of depth and details when I read this way. My daily question is **What does today look like for me?** My cards usually give me the information I need. When I need more detail I keep pulling until I get what I need from the reading. Anything goes when you are the one making the rules!

Major Arcana

	UPRIGHT	REVERSED
THE FOOL 0	Beginnings, innocence, spontaneous, free spirited	Indecision, hesitation, recklessness, risk-taking
THE MAGICIAN I	Inspired action, manifestation, resourcefulness, power	Manipulation, poor planning, untapped talents
THE HIGH PRIESTESS II	Sacred knowledge, wisdom, intuition, divine feminine, subconscious mind	Secrets, withdrawal, silence, disconnected from intuition
THE EMPRESS III	Femininity, beauty, nature, nurturing, abundance	Creative block, dependence on others
THE EMPEROR IV (ARIES)	Structure, authority, establishment, father-figure	Excessive control, domination, inflexible, undisciplined
THE HIEROPHANT V (TAURUS)	Religious beliefs, spiritual wisdom, conformity, tradition, institutions	Personal beliefs, freedom, unorthodoxy
THE LOVERS VI (GEMINI)	Love, relationships, harmony, aligned values, choices	Imbalance, disharmony, self-love
THE CHARIOT VII (CANCER)	Control, willpower, success, action, determination	Self-discipline, opposition, lack of direction
STRENGTH VIII (LEO)	Courage, persuasion, strength, influence, action	Inner strength, self-doubt, low energy, raw emotion
THE HERMIT IX (VIRGO)	Soul searching, introspection, aloneness, inner guidance	Isolation, loneliness, withdrawal
THE WHEEL OF FORTUNE X	Good luck, karma, life cycles, destiny, a turning point	Cycle breaking, resistance to change, bad luck
JUSTICE XI (LIBRA)	Justice, fairness, truth, law, cause and effect	Dishonesty, unfairness, lack of accountability
THE HANGED MAN XII	New perspectives, pause, surrender, let go	Delays, resistance, stalling, indecision

Major Arcana

	UPRIGHT	REVERSED
DEATH XIII (*SCORPIO*)	Endings, change, transition transformation	Resistance to change, personal transformation, inner purging
TEMPERANCE XIV (*SAGITTARIUS*)	Balance, moderation, patience, purpose	Imbalance, excess, self-healing, realignment
THE DEVIL XV (*CAPRICORN*)	Shadow self, attachment, addiction, restriction, sexuality	Release limiting beliefs, exploring dark thoughts, detachment
THE TOWER XVI	Chaos, sudden change, upheaval, revelation, awakening	Personal transformation, fear of change, averting disaster
THE STAR XVII (*AQUARIUS*)	Hope, faith, purpose, renewal, spirituality	Lack of faith, despair, self-trust, disconnection
THE MOON XVIII (*PISCES*)	Subconscious, intuition, illusion, fear, anxiety	Release of fear, repressed emotion, inner confusion
THE SUN XIX	Positivity, fun, warmth, vitality, success	Inner child, feeling down, overly optimistic
JUDGMENT XX	Inner calling, rebirth, judgment, absolution	self-doubt, inner critic, ignoring the call
THE WORLD XXI	Completion, integration, accomplishment, travel	Seeking personal closure, short-cuts, delays

THE MAJOR ARCANA TELLS THE STORY OF SOUL'S JOURNEY THROUGH THE UNIVERSE. It answers the "Why" questions, and describes the lessons you need to learn. These cards represent your soul's progression on a life journey toward enlightenment, major life THEMES, and changes. Read only these to focus on spiritual matters.

A DOMINANTLY MAJOR ARCANA SPREAD demonstrates life-changing events with long-term effects and life lessons needed to progress.

Minor Arcana

Elemental association of the suits and what they symbolize

Cups (element = water): Emotions, creativity, intuition, relationships

Pentacles (element = earth): Material wealth, money, career, manifestation

Swords (element = air): Communication, truth, intellect, thoughts

Wands (element = fire): Inspiration, energy, enthusiasm

Numerological association of the cards

1 – (Aces) New beginnings, opportunity, potential

2 – Balance, partnership, duality

3 – Creativity, groups, growth

4 – Structure, stability, manifestation

5 – Change, instability, conflict

6 – Communication, cooperation, harmony

7 – Reflection, assessment, knowledge

8 – Mastery, action, accomplishment

9 – Fruition, attainment, fulfilment

10 – Completion, end of a cycle, renewal

THE MINOR ARCANA DESCRIBES THE UNIVERSE THAT YOUR SOUL IS JOURNEYING THROUGH. It describes the forces that surround you, the situations and events you find yourself in, and the free will and lessons learned in daily life. These are the DETAILS of life or a roadmap forward.

A DOMINANTLY MINOR ARCANA SPREAD demonstrates more practical, day-to-day issues. NUMBERED CARDS refer to everyday situations. COURT CARDS refer to actual people or personality types.

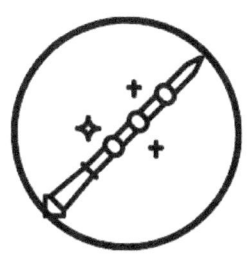

Wands

	UPRIGHT	REVERSED
ACE OF WANDS	Inspiration, new opportunities, growth, potential	Emerging idea, lack of direction, distraction, delays
TWO OF WANDS	Future planning, progress, decisions, discovery	Personal goals, inner alignment, fear of unknown, lack of planning
THREE OF WANDS	Foresight, progress, expansion, opportunity overseas	Playing small, lacking foresight, unexpected delays
FOUR OF WANDS	Celebration, joy, homecoming, harmony, relaxation	Personal celebration, harmony within, tension, conflict with others
FIVE OF WANDS	Disagreement, conflict, competition, tension, diversity	Inner conflict, conflict avoidance, release of tension
SIX OF WANDS	Success, recognition, progress, self-confidence	Personal success, private achievement, fall from grace, egotism
SEVEN OF WANDS	Challenge, competition, protection, perseverance	Giving up, exhaustion, feeling overwhelmed
EIGHT OF WANDS	Fast-paced change, movement, action, alignment, air travel	Frustration, delays, resisting change, internal alignment
NINE OF WANDS	Resilience, courage, persistence, test of faith, boundaries	Inner resources, struggle, overwhelm, defensive, paranoia
TEN OF WANDS	Burden, extra responsibility, hard work, completion	Doing it all, delegation, release, carrying the burden
PAGE OF WANDS	Inspiration, ideas, discovery, limitless potential, free spirit	Newly formed ideas, redirecting energy, self-limiting beliefs, spiritual path
KNIGHT OF WANDS	Energy, passion, inspired action, adventure, impulsiveness	Passion project, haste, scattered energy, frustration, delays
QUEEN OF WANDS	Courage, confidence, independence, determination, social butterfly	Self-respect, self-confidence, introverted, re-establish sense of self
KING OF WANDS	Natural born leader, vision, entrepreneur, honor	Impulsiveness, haste, ruthlessness, high expectations

FIRE ELEMENT: Inspiration, energy, enthusiasm, movement, passion.

TIMING: burns fast (Think days). ADVICE: Protect your interests.

	UPRIGHT	REVERSED
ACE OF CUPS	Love, new relationships, passion, creativity	Self-love, intuition, repressed emotions
TWO OF CUPS	Unified love, partnership, mutual attraction	Self-love, break-up, disharmony, distrust
THREE OF CUPS	Celebration, friendship, creativity, collaboration	Independence, alone time, hardcore partying, three's a crowd
FOUR OF CUPS	Meditation, contemplation, reality, reevaluation	Retreat, withdrawal, check into alignment
FIVE OF CUPS	Regret, failure, disappointment, pessimism	Personal setbacks, self-forgiveness, moving on
SIX OF CUPS	Revisiting the past, childhood memories, innocence, joy	Living in the past, forgiveness, lack of playfulness
SEVEN OF CUPS	Opportunities, choices, wishful thinking, illusion	Alignment, personal values, overwhelmed by choices
EIGHT OF CUPS	Disappointment, abandonment, withdrawal, escapism	Trying one more time, indecision, aimless drifting, walking away
NINE OF CUPS	Contentment, satisfaction, gratitude, wish come true	Inner happiness, materialism, dissatisfaction, indulgence
TEN OF CUPS	Divine love, blissful relationships, harmony, alignment.	Disconnection, misaligned values, struggling relationships
PAGE OF CUPS	Creative opportunities, intuitive messages, curiosity, possibility	New ideas, doubting intuition, creative blocks, emotional immaturity
KNIGHT OF CUPS	Creativity, romance, charm, imagination, beauty	Overactive imagination, unrealistic, jealous, moody
QUEEN OF CUPS	Compassionate, caring, emotionally stable, intuitive, in flow	Inner feelings, self-care, self-love, co-dependency
KING OF CUPS	Emotionally balanced, compassionate, diplomatic	Self compassion, inner feelings, moodiness, emotionally manipulative

WATER ELEMENT: Emotions, creativity, intuition, relationships.

TIMING: ebbs with the moon (Think months). ADVICE: Listen to your intuition.

Swords

	UPRIGHT	REVERSED
ACE OF SWORDS	Breakthroughs, new ideas, mental clarity, success	Inner clarity, rethinking an idea, clouded judgment
TWO OF SWORDS	Difficult decisions, weighing options, an impasse, avoidance	Indecision, confusion, information overload, stalemate
THREE OF SWORDS	Heartbreak, emotional pain, sorrow, grief, hurt	Negative self talk, releasing pain, optimism, forgiveness
FOUR OF SWORDS	Rest, relaxation, meditation, contemplation, recuperation	Exhaustion, burnout, deep contemplation, stagnation
FIVE OF SWORDS	Conflict, disagreement, competition, defeat, win at all costs	Past resentment, making amends, reconciliation
SIX OF SWORDS	Transition, change, rite of passage, release baggage	Personal transition, unfinished business, resistant to change
SEVEN OF SWORDS	Betrayal, deception, getting away with something, acting strategically	Self-deceit, imposter syndrome, keeping secrets
EIGHT OF SWORDS	Negative thoughts self-imposed restriction, imprisonment, victim mentality	Self-limiting beliefs, inner critic, releasing negative thoughts, open to new perspectives
NINE OF SWORDS	Anxiety, worry, fear, depression, nightmares	Inner turmoil, deep-seated fear, secrets, releasing worry
TEN OF SWORDS	Painful endings, deep wounds, betrayal, loss, crisis	Recovery, regeneration, resisting an inevitable end
PAGE OF SWORDS	New ideas, curiosity, thirst for knowledge, new ways of communication	Self-expression, all talk-no action, haphazard action, haste
KNIGHT OF SWORDS	Ambitious, action-oriented, driven to succeed, fast thinking	Restless, unfocused, impulsive, burnout
QUEEN OF SWORDS	Independent, unbiased judgment, clear boundaries, direct communication	Overly emotional, easily influenced, spiteful, cold-hearted
KING OF SWORDS	Mental clarity, intellectual power, authority, truth	Quiet power, inner truth, misuse of power, manipulation

AIR ELEMENT: Communication, truth, intellect, thoughts, logic.
TIMING: flows quickly (Think week). ADVICE: Make plans and release worry.

 # Pentacles

	UPRIGHT	REVERSED
ACE OF PENTACLES	New financial or career opportunity, manifestation, abundance	Lost opportunity, lack of planning and foresight
TWO OF PENTACLES	Multiple priorities, time management, prioritization, adaptability	Overcommitted, disorganization, reprioritization
THREE OF PENTACLES	Teamwork, collaboration, learning, implementation	Disharmony, misalignment, working alone
FOUR OF PENTACLES	Saving money, security, conservative, scarcity, control	Overspending, greed, self-protection
FIVE OF PENTACLES	Financial loss, poverty, lack mindset, isolation, worry	Recovery from financial loss, spiritual poverty
SIX OF PENTACLES	Giving, receiving, sharing wealth, generosity, charity	Self-care, unpaid debts, one-sided charity
SEVEN OF PENTACLES	Long-term view, sustainable results, perseverance, investments	Lack of long-term vision, limited success or reward
EIGHT OF PENTACLES	Apprenticeship, repetitive tasks, mastery, skill development	Self-development, perfectionism, misdirected activity
NINE OF PENTACLES	Abundance, luxury, self-sufficiency, financial independence	Self-worth, over-investment in work, hustling
TEN OF PENTACLES	Wealth, financial security, family, long-term success, contribution	The dark side of wealth, financial failure or loss
PAGE OF PENTACLES	Manifestation, financial opportunity, skill development	Lack of progress, procrastination, learning from failure
KNIGHT OF PENTACLES	Hard work, productivity, routine, conservatism	Self-discipline, boredom, stuck in a rut, perfectionism
QUEEN OF PENTACLES	Nurturing, practical, providing financially, working parent	Financial independence, self-care, work-home conflict
KING OF PENTACLES	Wealth, business, leadership, security, discipline, abundance	Financial ineptitude, obsession with wealth and status, stubborn

EARTH ELEMENT: Material wealth, career, manifestation, practicality, business, education.

TIMING: grows slowly (Think a season to a year). ADVICE: Use common sense.

Birth Cards

THESE CARDS DESCRIBE A FACET OF THE SELF THAT IS CONSTANT.
THEY CAN SHOW YOUR PATH

STEP ONE: Reduce your birthday to numbers. March 12, 1977 becomes: MM DD YY YY 03 12 19 77	**STEP TWO:** Add these numbers together. 3 + 12 + 19 + 77 = 111
STEP THREE: When a sum is 3 digits, add the first 2 to the third. 11 + 1 = 12 *(This is your first birth card)* Now add these 2 together. 1 + 2 = 3 *(This is your second birth card)*	The first birth card corresponds to the **Major Arcana # 10-21** The second birth card is the sum of the 2 digits and corresponds to **Major Arcana #1-10**
FIRST BIRTH CARD:	SECOND BIRTH CARD:

Personal Signifier

This card is chosen based on intuition and connection and can change based on your feelings or reading. If this card shows up you could be reading for someone similar to you in some way. It can also tell you that something is off with your personally that is interfering with your reading. When reading for yourself, it's a message that you're getting in your own way. Take a beat, stop analyzing, and get away from the cards.

Shadow Card

The base card in a deck alludes to hidden aspects influencing the situation, deep insight into the subconscious mind of the subject, or the crux of the matter. It can tell you the reason the reading is being carried out.

Significators

A SIGNIFICATOR OR SIGNIFIER IS A CARD THAT IS CONSCIOUSLY CHOSEN TO REPRESENT THE QUERENT OR THE SITUATION THEY ARE ASKING ABOUT.

THE FOOL	New beginnings	THE STAR	Hopes and wishes
THE MAGICIAN	Trickery and enterprise	THE MOON	Uncertainty
THE HIGH PRIESTESS	Psychic ability	THE SUN	Happiness and family
THE EMPRESS	Parenthood	JUDGMENT	Destiny and life's calling
THE EMPEROR	Career advancement	THE WORLD	Travel and world issues
THE HIEROPHANT	Religion and leaders	WANDS	Work and business
THE LOVERS	Love and choice	CUPS	Love, family, and relationships
THE CHARIOT	Fame and achievement	SWORDS	Strife or logic
STRENGTH	Courage and strength	PENTACLES	Finances or health
THE HERMIT	Self-discovery		
THE WHEEL OF FORTUNE	luck		
JUSTICE	Law, equality, and morals		
THE HANGED MAN	Health		
DEATH	Life changing decisions		
TEMPERANCE	Peace and happiness		
THE DEVIL	Addiction and obsession		
THE TOWER	Chaos and shock		

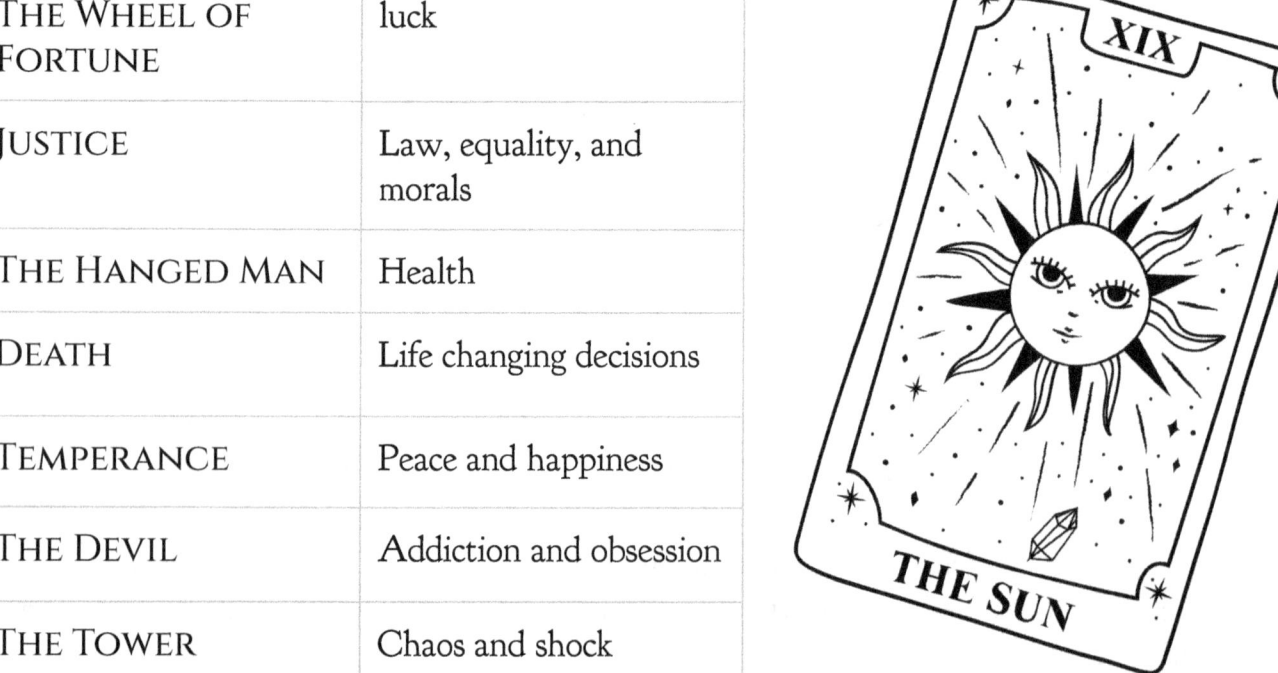

XIX

THE SUN

Tips & Tricks

SOMETHING NOT GOING YOUR WAY?
Find the Wheel of Fortune in the deck. Two cards on either side are the solution to your problem.

TO BRING FORTH MONEY...
Pull the 1st, 5th, 10th, 20th, and 50th card. They will tell you how.

TO FIND THE ROOT OF ROMANTIC CONFLICT...
Find The Lovers. The cards on either side are the conflicts surrounding the relationship.

TO LEAVE BEHIND SADNESS...
Find The Moon and Sun cards. The number of cards in between represent the number of steps you must take.

TO LOOK INTO YOUR FUTURE...
Find your nearest birth card. The card beneath is what approaching soonest.

QUESTION STEMS FOR SINGLE CARD DRAW
What is the energy surrounding...
What is the meaning/lesson of...
What's going on when...
What are the underlying circumstances of...
What do I need to know about...
How do I get along better with...
How do I reconnect with...
How might I...
How can I resolve...
How can I advance...
How can I improve...(my chances, my relationship, my ability)
How can I transition from...to...
What role do I play in...
What can I do to...
What must I change to...

YES AND NO QUESTIONS

Wands = yes, but it will require work on your part

Cups= yes. It will come to you naturally

Pentacles = It will come to you at a price

Swords= Absolutely not

Major Arcana=Good luck and be careful

Key Card Indicators

LOVE

The Lovers- unique bond, deep connection
The Empress- sensuality within the relationship
The Emperor- long term partner
Hierophant- committed, traditional relationship
Ace of Cups- new relationships, joy, excitement
2 of Cups- strong bond, commitment
4 of Wands- celebration, safe and secure home
10 of Cups- happy family, loving home
10 of Pentacles- well established relationship
Knight of Cups- courted, romanced, special

SEX

The Devil- great sex, something amiss
Temperance- opposites attract, balance
The Star- tantric, highly spiritual sex
Ace of Pentacles- fertile union, use protection
Ace of Wands- things are going well
3 of Cups- fun, menage a trois
4 of Swords- passive and routine sex
8 of Wands- quick and dirty sex
8 of Swords- bondage and sado-masochism
Knight of Wands- flirty, passion with lust

CHEATING

The Magician (rev.)- taking advantage of you
The High Priestess (reversed)- a mistress
Judgment (rev.)- refuse responsibility for actions
The Devil- partner is giving into temptation
The Tower- fallout after an affair
The Moon (rev.)- secrets, things yet revealed
3 of Cups (reversed)- presence of a 3rd party
7 of Swords- think they've gotten away with it
8 of Cups- trying to avoid consequences
10 of Swords (reversed)- betrayal

BREAK-UPS

The Hermit- solitude and alone time
Death- time to let go, embrace future
The Tower- turmoil
2 of Cups (reversed)- best to break
3 of Cups- love triangle, unfaithful partner
3 of Swords- grief, sorrow, heartbreak
5 of Swords- a battle lost
5 of Pentacles- isolated and shut out
10 of Swords- painful, unexpected, dramatic end
10 of Pentacles (reversed)- assets divested

ABUSIVE RELATIONSHIPS

The Emperor (rev.)- insecure, needs control
The Devil- bound, but freedom is possible
The Moon (rev.)- subtle abuse, victim unaware
The Chariot (rev.)- anger issues, potential
violence
5 of Swords- victim psychological abuse, bullying
8 of Swords- trapped, unable to see a way out
9 of Swords- conflict and arguments
9 of Wands- physical, mental abuse
10 of Swords- abuse reflects betrayal, deception
King of Swords (rev.)- not a nice guy

CONFLICT/TENSION

The Chariot (rev.)- 2 headstrong people at odds
Temperance (rev.)- harmony gives way to conflict
and tension
The Tower- absolute destruction and chaos
2 of Swords- passive aggressive conflict
2 of Cups (rev.)- once beautiful relationship
becomes all out war
3 of Swords- hurtful words inflict emotional pain
5 of Swords- tried to win, lost trust/relationship
5 of Wands- lots of shouting, no one listening
7 of Wands- under threat of attack
9 of Wands- perseverance in aftermath

GUILT/SHAME	DELAYS/WAITING
Judgment (reversed)- regret past actions, guilty The Devil-engaged in self-destructive behavior 2 of Swords- in denial 5 of Cups- regret and shame 5 of Swords (reversed)- learn from experience 6 of Wands (reversed)- actions lake you look bad 7 of Swords (rev.)- ashamed deceived others/self 9 of Swords- huge stress/anxiety over actions 9 of Wands- paranoid about acting dishonest 10 of Wands- time to let go of baggage	The Hanged Man- waiting/contemplating The Hermit (reversed)- plans on hold/reassess The Chariot (reversed)-delays because of others 2 of Swords- failure to choose=delays 3 of Wands (rev)- realign expectations, new path 4 of Cups- self delay, reflect on your desires 4 of Swords- rest and relax 7 of Pentacles- moving forward at a slow pace 8 of Wands (rev)- frustration, delay, no progress Ace of Wands (rev.)- unexpected delays mean a blessing in disguise

FINANCES/MONEY	MENTAL ILLNESS
The Sun- positive outcome, high earning The Wheel of Fortune- good luck, surprise gifts 4 of Pentacles- spend less, save more 6 of Wands- rewarded for hard work 7 of Pentacles- long term rewards from investing 9 of Cups- laws of attraction 9 of Pentacles- material abundance, luxury 10 of Pentacles- amassed wealth can be shared Page of Pentacles- adventure, chance to earn Ace of Pentacles- new opportunity	The Devil- addiction, unhealthy attachment The Moon (rev.)- general mental health issues haven't been explored Temperance (rev.)- possible chemical imbalance The Tower- breakdown, crisis, panic attacks The Star (rev.)- lack of faith, hopelessness 5 of Cups (rev.)- depression due to loss 5 of Pentacles- anxiety due to finances 9 of Cups (rev.)- emotional needs not being met 9 of Swords- anxiety, depression spurred by negative self talk 9 of Wands (rev.)-paranoia, feeling all is against

SUCCESS/ACHIEVEMENT	HEALING
The Sun- success The World- achievement The Emperor- structured/dedicated approach The Chariot- overcome barriers to find success 4 of Wands- bask in success, celebrate milestones 6 of Wands- in spotlight, positive role model 9 of Pentacles- independent, well versed in financial matters 10 of Pentacles- you will have what you desire 10 of Cups- highest love and harmony in relationships King of Wands- culmination, accumulation, achievement	Death- acknowledge something has ended The Star- universe is with us in good and bad The Hermit- encourages personal journey of introspection Temperance- healing can be a long process, but every step helps Judgment- we learn and move forward 3 of Cups- friends/loved ones support us healing 4 of Swords- need time and space to heal 5 of Cups- forgiveness allows us to trust/love again 6 of Swords- keep moving forward Ace of Cups- don't be afraid, let emotions flow

Deck Dedication

Tarot cards are sacred tools that act as our conduit to Spirit. To bless, consecrate, or dedicate a deck to a specific purpose enhances their ability to work with us in that vein. It also deepens our connection to our cards because it declares a partnership. I'm including ideas here, but I urge you to make them your own. Your intuition will guide you on the best way to do this for your practice.

START WITH A FRESHLY CLEANSED DECK!

BLESSING

Create a sacred space, light a candle, focus on the energy coming from the flame and visualize that power in your deck as light. Focus on this energy for a moment and say, **"Bless this deck to illuminate the path, enlighten and empower me to share wisdom and guidance to those who seek."**

CONSECRATION

As you make a circle of salt around your work space say, **"With the element of Earth I banish negative energy and create a protected space to work"**. Wet the tips of your fingers with water and brush the deck including the edges and say, **"With the element of water I purify this deck of all unwanted energy"**. Pass the deck through incense smoke and say, **"With the elements of Air and Fire I charge this deck with wisdom and healing"**. If you work with a specific spiritual power you can incorporate that here. **"May the element of Spirit radiate within and without and bless these sacred cards with the power of Truth." Spirit, Fire, Air, Water and Earth, you were here and I thank you. The circle is open, but never unbroken. As I speak, so shall it be.** After your deck has been consecrated, you may choose to invoke a deity, element, ancestor, guide, angel or saint you work with.

DEDICATION

Think about your "why". What is your intention for this deck? How do you plan to use it? What are your hopes for working with it? These answers are your dedication. Write it down if that helps you. Next you are going to mark the deck as your own. To do this you can hold it to your heart or third eye, use a pencil to mark the edge of the deck, breathe on the deck, kiss or even whisper to your cards. Now speak your dedication to your cards.

Grounding Exercise

GROUNDING IS NECESSARY FOR ANY
SPIRITUAL WORK BECAUSE IT BRINGS
BALANCE TO MIND, BODY, AND SOUL.

We need that balance to be able to interpret the wisdom we are being entrusted with to give guidance to others. Grounding does not have to be a difficult exercise. It is about breathing, relaxing, and opening ourselves up to Spirit.

I find that NATURE is the easiest way for me to ground, but do what feels right to you. Walk barefoot. Sit on the ground. Shower or take a bath. Stand in the rain. Sit on the beach and watch the waves. Watch a thunderstorm. Be out in the wind. Sit next to a fire. Focus on a candle flame. Watch incense smoke. Soak up the sunshine.

You need a space where you won't be interrupted and you can remove distractions. TAKE A DEEP BREATH AND EXHALE. Repeat this a few times until you are breathing evenly and regularly. Now it's time to focus on energy. You can do this by rubbing your hands together as though warming them and feeling the tingling sensation that builds there. THAT IS ENERGY. Close your eyes, focus, and feel it. Visualize that energy coursing through your body as you center yourself. This will get easier with each time you do it until it becomes second nature.

Now that you're centered you can ground. Grounding allows us to MOVE ENERGY out of ourselves and into the Earth. We then funnel the Earth's energy back into ourselves. I like to be standing or sitting on the ground for this VISUALIZATION. See yourself as a tree with a root system. Focus all your energy and growing your roots as deep as they will go. Follow them to the center of the core where you will see the Earth's energy as light or fire. When you have connected to that energy, visualize it travelling back up through the root system to you.

YOU ARE CENTERED AND SAFE.
YOU ARE STRONG AND GROUNDED.
YOU ARE PROTECTED BY MOTHER EARTH.

Intuition Exercises

INTUITION IS AN UNCONSCIOUS AWARENESS OR WISDOM THAT CAN'T ALWAYS BE EXPLAINED.

It's that feeling that you just know, though you can't explain how you know exactly. You're not crazy...It's just your intuition pointing things out that your physical self can't detect. The cool part is that you can strengthen your intuition by being mindful. Here are a few strategies to do just that.

- **Be present for yourself.** Check in regularly about how you feel. It's important to slow down and listen your inner voice.
- **Meditate.** Meditation is such a powerful tool because it can shift our awareness.
- **Journal, journal, journal!** I cannot stress this one enough. Putting your thoughts on paper is an essential key to staying tuned in with yourself.
- **Prioritize your intuition over data.** Make time to think things through and allow your intuition to work. Sit with your feelings before taking action.
- **Identify how your intuition speaks to you.** Does your information come to you as visions, thoughts, music lyrics, gut feelings, shivers up your spine?
- **Keep track of your dreams.** Dreams can tell us what is going on deep within us because it is how your subconscious mind communicates with your conscious mind.
- **Pay attention to your other 5 senses.** The more conscious you are about acknowledging the other 5, the sooner the 6th will kick in.
- **Find a creative pursuit.** Creativity quiets the cognitive mind and allows intuition to work.
- **Check your hunches.** Start writing your hunches down and see how often you're right.
- **Pay attention to your body.** What physical feelings accompany your intuition? Even Buffy the vampire slayer got cramps whenever a vamp was near. That's intuition folks.
- **Slow down and breathe.** Sometimes we have to stop hustling and be still in order to access our intuition.
- **Be in nature as often as you can.** Take a walk in the woods. Lie in the sun. Listen to the wind chime on your porch. Nature is a mad powerful trigger for intuition.
- **Look back over your past.** I'll bet there were a lot of things that you saw coming. Can you see the patterns?
- **Feeling is just as important as thinking.** The mind can be fearful, but the intuition can always be trusted. Check yourself. Are you thinking or feeling?
- **Get up and move.** Repetitive movement triggers intuition. I get the big intuitive wisdom when I am washing dishes for some reason. Try any action that you can do on auto-pilot.

Tarot Meditation

TAROT CAN BE A SACRED TOOL FOR GUIDANCE AS WELL AS A SELF-AWARENESS PRACTICE.

Whether you are working toward reading for people or you want a new way to practice mindfulness, meditation can make a difference in your tarot practice. Meditation is defined as a practice in which an individual uses a technique – such as focusing the mind on a particular object, thought, or activity – to train attention and awareness, and achieve a mentally clear and emotionally calm and stable state.

YOU WILL NEED:

A calm, quiet place without disruptions where you can sit comfortably. Candles or incense can boost your mood for meditation. Music helps me relax, but stick to something that won't pull your focus. Think spa-tunes rather than rock concert.

1. Take a deep breath and exhale. Repeat this a few times until your breathing is even and relaxed. Observe your breathing throughout this exercise.
2. Think about your 'why'. What is your reason for this exercise?
3. Pull a card from your deck. What is it?
4. Is it Major Arcana (Themes) or Minor Arcana (Details)?
5. What is the elemental association?
6. What do you see? Look for the literal and obvious things. No detail is too small here. The goal is to trigger your subconscious to make connections to your own life experiences.
7. What connections can you make to what you see on the card?
8. Imagine yourself as a character on the card. How can you relate?
9. What other thoughts and feelings do you get?
10. Record your interpretation and reflections about the card.

Tarot reading is a skill that grows with practice, time, and commitment. This meditation can really spark your intuition and give you a deeply personal way to learn card meanings that goes beyond rote memorization. Some people have more inherent intuitive capability than others, but we all have the ability to strengthen our intuition with exercise.

Intention Prompts:

HERE ARE A FEW QUESTIONS TO HELP YOU THINK ABOUT SETTING INTENTIONS FOR WHEN YOU NEED A LITTLE HELP

1. What have I been neglecting?

2. What does my heart need?

3. What opportunity should I take?

4. How can I connect with friends and family?

5. What have I been holding on to?

6. What am I afraid of?

7. I am grateful for?

8. What can you forgive yourself for? Someone else?

9. What do you love about yourself?

10. What is one thing to focus on this lunar cycle?

11. What do I want to create more of in my life?

12. Where am I craving change?

13. Where am I afraid to change?

14. What do I want more/less of?

15. What's working/not working for me?

16. What energy do I want to embody this month

17. Where have I strayed from my vision/path?

18. How can I grow?

19. What are my hopes, dreams, and wishes?

20. What fresh start would I like to make?

21. How can I cleanse my life?

22. Where do I want to improve my effort?

23. What are you struggling with?

24. What trauma are you hanging onto?

25. If success is guaranteed, what would you try?

The "Me" Page

It's really easy to get caught up in the pressure of life and who the world thinks we are "supposed" to be. Sometimes we forget all about who we actually are, or who we want to be. Take your time and be honest with this activity. On the days when you feel like you don't recognize yourself, it will be here with all of your answers to remind you just who you are.

THINGS I LIKE: _____

_____

_____

_____

_____

_____

I GET EXCITED ABOUT:_____

_____

_____

_____

_____

_____

THINGS I WANT TO DO OR LEARN:_____

_____

_____

_____

_____

_____

PLACES I WANT TO GO:_____

_____

_____

_____

_____

_____

WHO I WANT TO BE WHEN I GROW UP: _____

_____

_____

_____

_____

Interview your deck

```
            ┌─────────┐
            │         │
            │         │
            │         │
            └─── 1 ───┘
    ┌─────────┐   ┌─────────┐
    │         │   │         │
    │         │   │         │
    │         │   │         │
    └─── 2 ───┘   └─── 3 ───┘
┌─────────┐ ┌─────────┐ ┌─────────┐
│         │ │         │ │         │
│         │ │         │ │         │
│         │ │         │ │         │
└─── 4 ───┘ └─── 5 ───┘ └─── 6 ───┘
```

1. Please introduce yourself: _____

_____

_____

2. Your strength as a deck?_____

_____

_____

3. Your limitations as a deck?_____

_____

_____

4. What can I learn from you?_____

_____

_____

5. What is the best way to work with you?_____

_____

_____

6. Outcome of your relationship with me?_____

_____

_____

Three Card Spread

Past / Present / Future

Mind / Body / Spirit

Stop/Start / Continue

Situation / Action / Outcome

The nature of your problem / The cause / The solution

Current situation / Obstacle / Advice

Context of the situation / Where you need to focus / Outcome

What I think about the situation / What I feel / What I do

Where you stand now / What you aspire to / How to get there

What you aspire to / What is standing in your way / How you can overcome this

What will help you / What will hinder you / What is your unrealised potential

What you can change / What you can't change / What you may not be aware of

What worked well / What didn't work well / Key learnings

You / The other person / The relationship

What brings you together / What pulls you apart / What needs your attention

Strengths / Weaknesses / Advice

Opportunities / Challenges / Outcome

Option 1 / Option 2 / Option 3

Option 1 / Option 2 / What you need to know to make a decision

The solution / An alternative solution / How to choose

Your conscious mind / Your subconscious mind / Your super-conscious mind

Material state / Emotional state / Spiritual state

You / Your current path / Your potential

What the Universe wants you to be / The personal qualities required / Specific action required

What you want (from the relationship) / What they want/ Where relationship is heading

Daily draw: Key focus / Emotional / Physical

Shadow work: The prison / The reason / The release

Weekly check-in: What is energizing me/Where can I expect to need grace/What should I look closer at

Balance: Where am I not putting enough energy/Where am I putting too much energy/How do I create balance

Four Card Spread

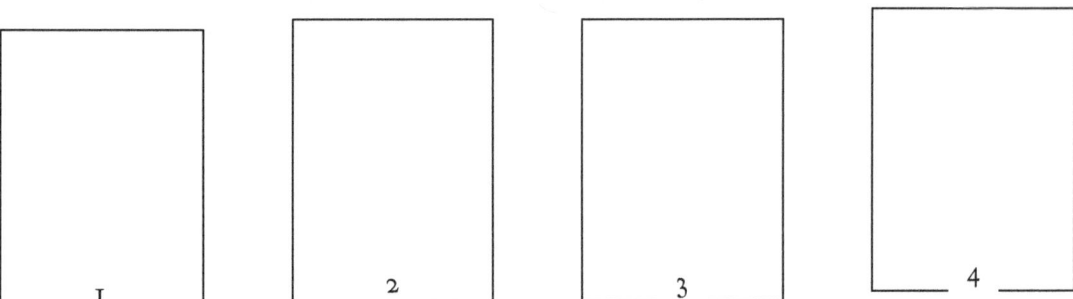

FOR GROUNDING

1. Where have you felt lost or insecure?
2. What helps you feel solid and confident?
3. Where do you find your strength?
4. What is a first step you can take towards grounding?

PERSONAL FOCUS

1. What do I need to think about?
2. What do I need to do?
3. What is my challenge?
4. What is my secret weapon?

REDUCE STRESS

1. My current reality
2. How can I center myself?
3. The best way for me to relax
4. How can I stop worrying about the future?

HEART MEDICINE

1. What does my heart need from me right now?
2. How can I give my heart what it needs?
3. Who has a message of love for me today?
4. What is that message?

DATING

1. Physical connection
2. Mental connection
3. Spiritual/Emotional connection
4. Long term potential

Five Card Spread

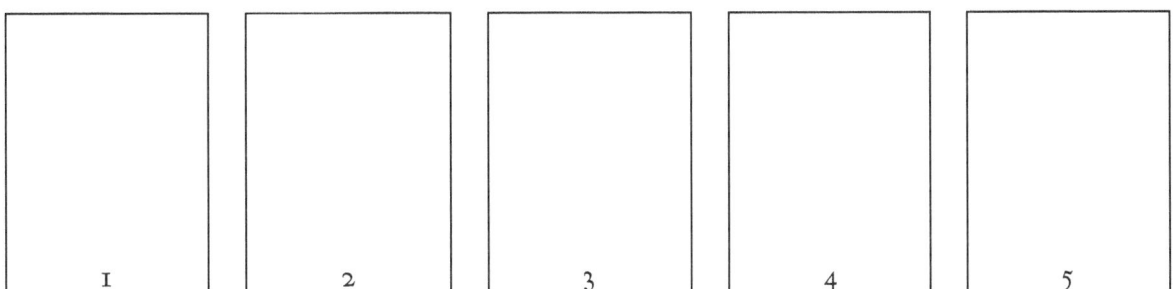

Need Advice?

1. You as you are

2. The correct path for you

3. The main obstacle

4. What is helping me?

5. How can progress be made?

Connecting With a Spirit Guide

1. Essence of your guide

2. A message your guide would like to convey that you have not been receptive to before

3. A reminder of what is important in this moment

4. How to be more open to messages from your guide in the future

5. What action you can take to honor and respect your guide

Simple Reading

1. Preconceived notions

2. The present

3. The unexpected

4. Near future

5. Distant future

Fork in the Road

1. The journey you are on

2. Option 1

3. How option 1 will turn out

4. Option 2

5. How option 2 will turn out

Wolf Paw Spread

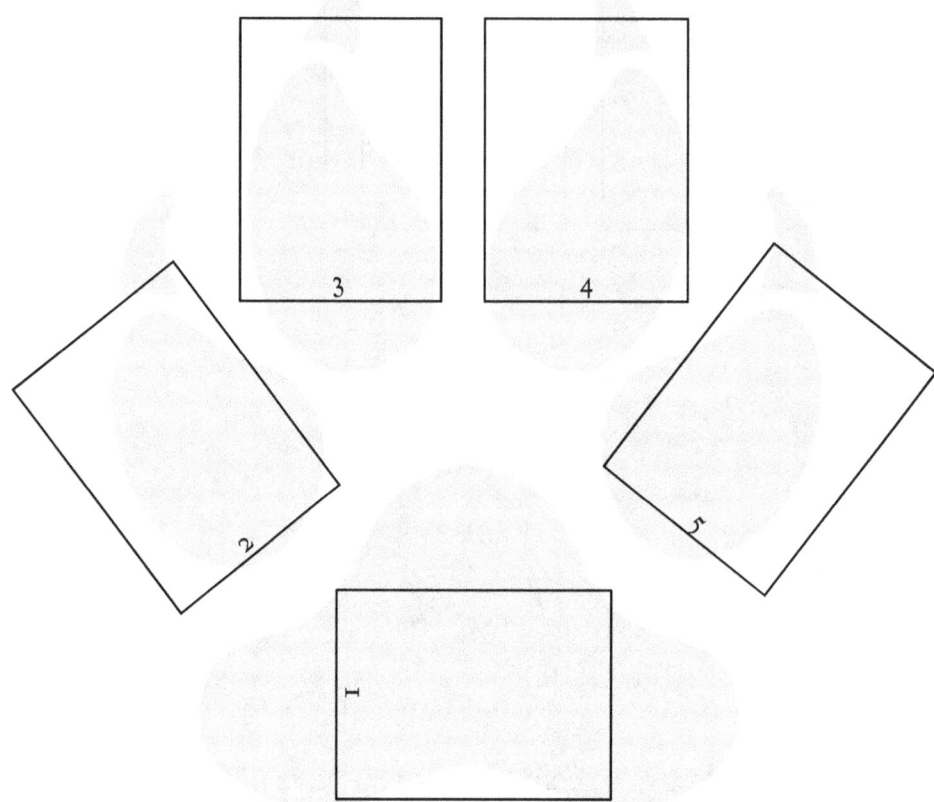

1. YOU. How can I strengthen and empower myself?

2. WORK. How can I pursue my work ambitions confidently?

3. SPIRIT. How can I nourish my spirit?

4. LOVE/RELATIONSHIPS. How can I deepen my pack bonds?

5. FAMILY. What does my pack need close to me?

Celtic Cross Spread

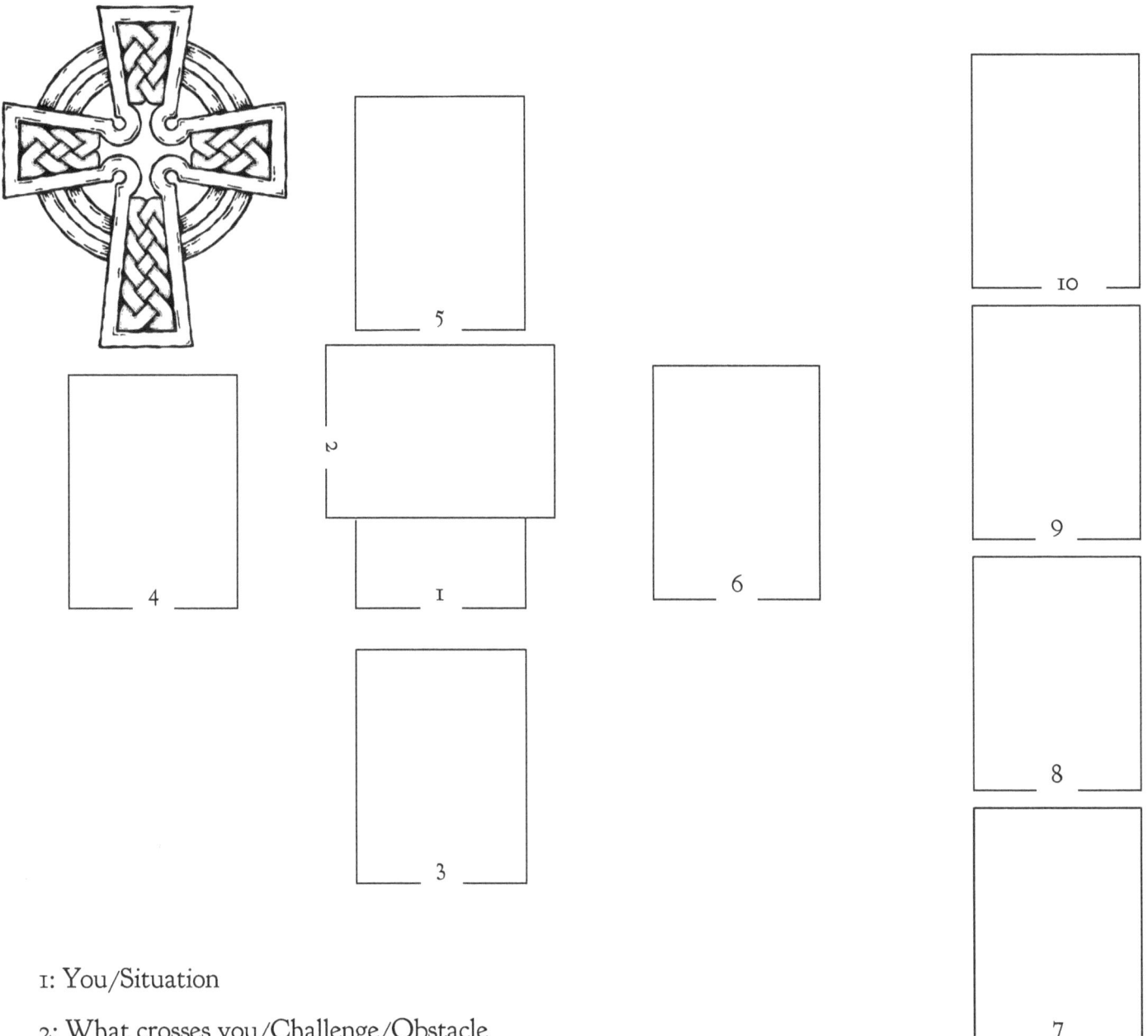

1: You/Situation

2: What crosses you/Challenge/Obstacle

3: What crowns you/Beliefs/Focus/Conscious

4: What is beneath you/Root/Subconscious/Recent Events

5: What is behind you/Past

6: What is before you/Future

7: Your Attitude/Power/Self-perception

8: Environment/Outside influences

9: Hopes/Fears/Action advice

10: Outcome

Compass Spread

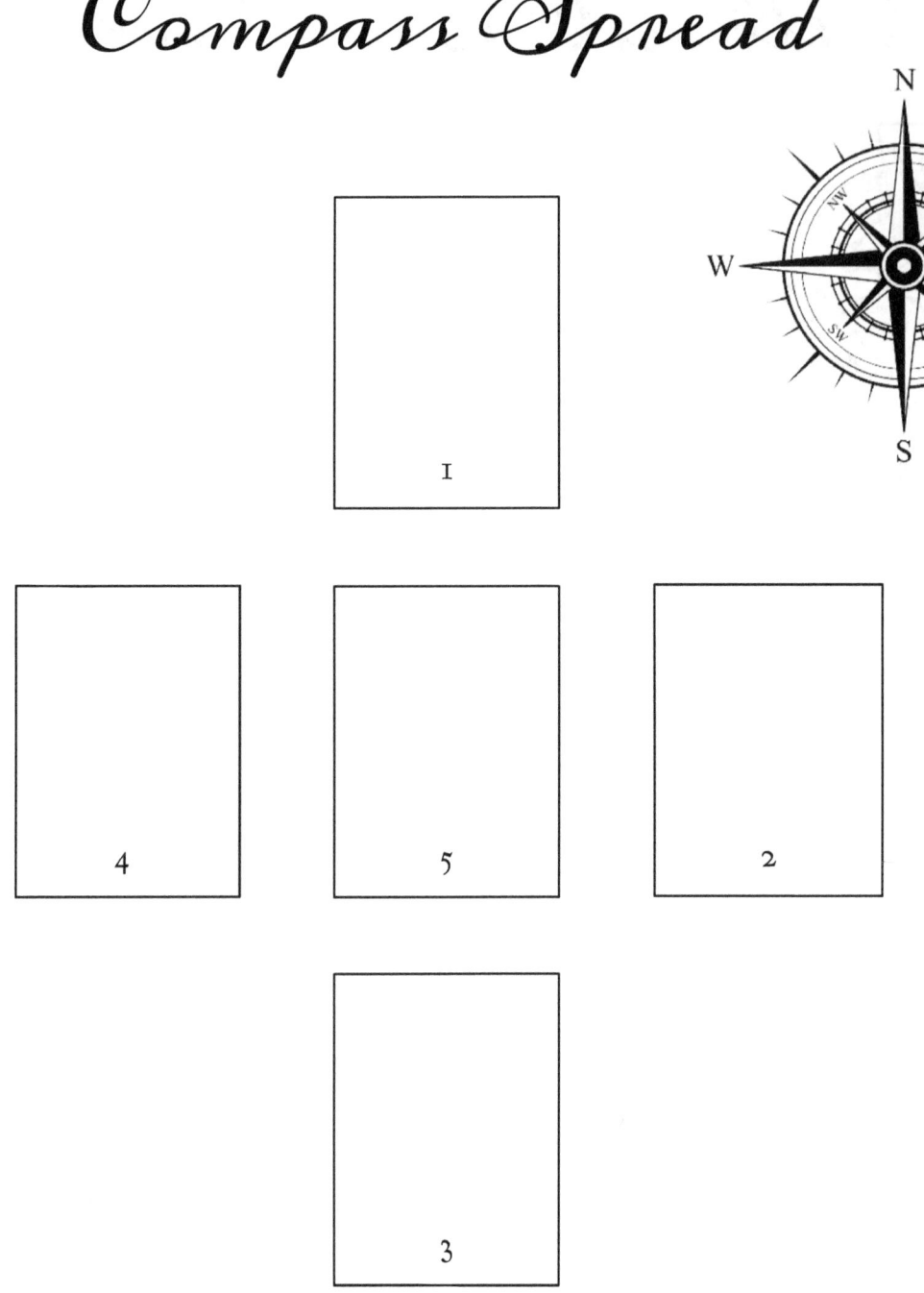

1. NORTH: Earth-What grounds you?

2. EAST: Air- What are your innermost thoughts?

3. SOUTH: Fire- What are you passionate about?

4. WEST: Water- What touches your heart?

5. SPIRIT- What defines you?

Break-up Spread

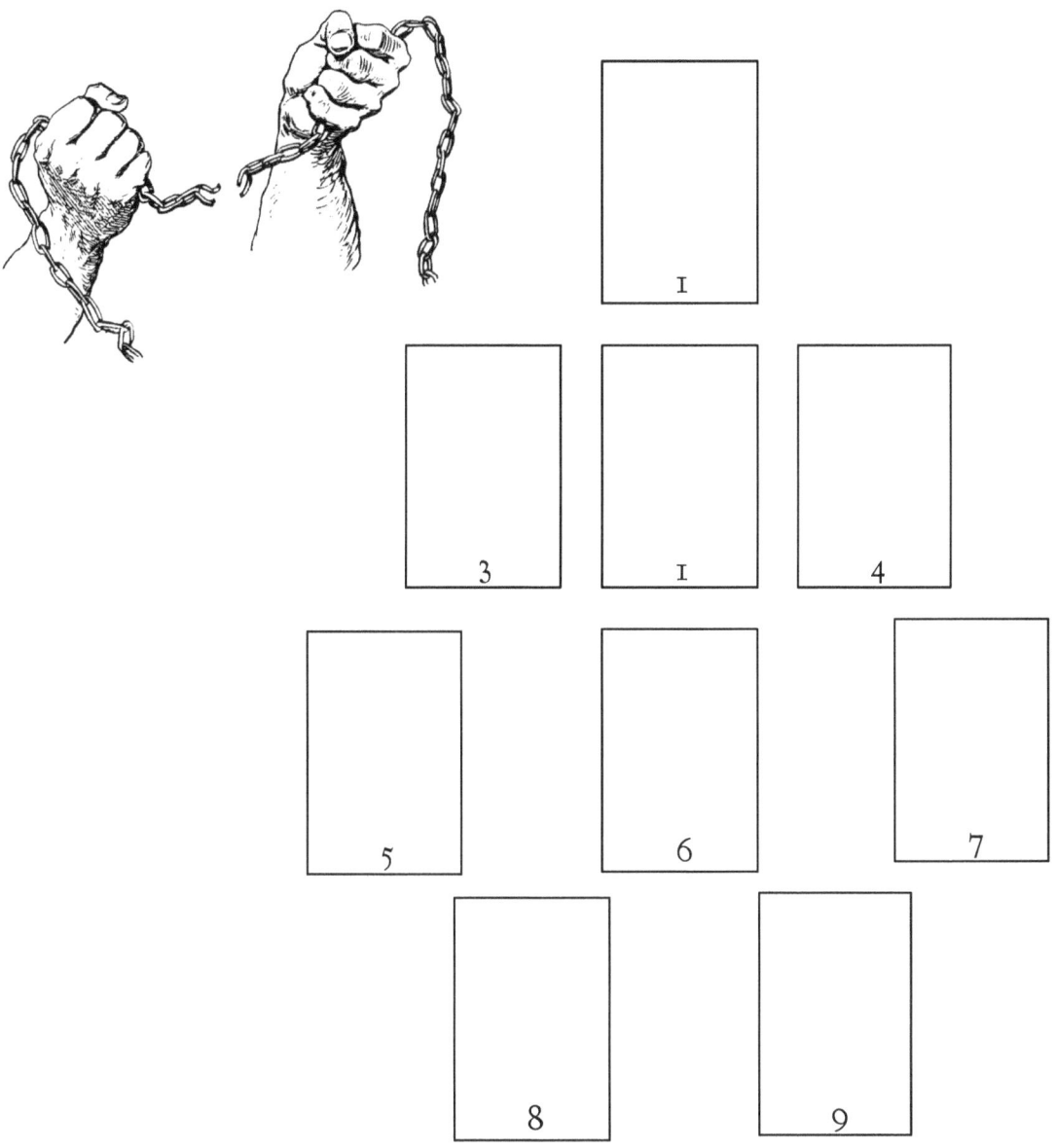

1. Why did this happen?

2. What lessons do I need to learn?

3. What positives can I take from this experience?

4. What action do I need to take to move forward?

5. What will help my heart mend?

6. What will help my mind mend?

7. What will help my soul mend?

8. What will help ground me?

9. Where do I go from here?

Facing Demons Spread

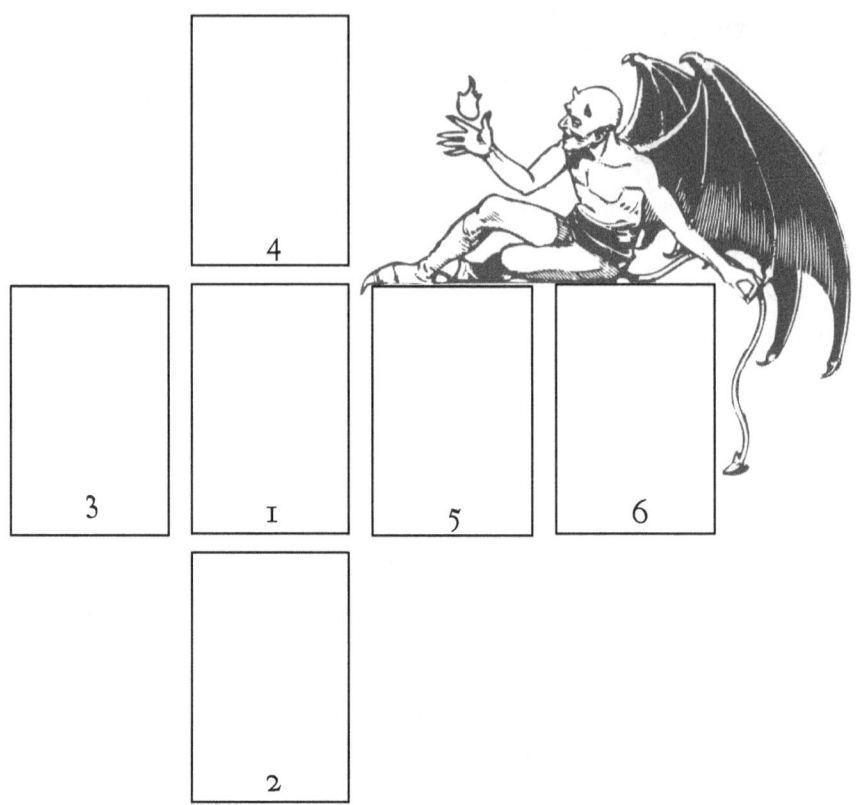

1. REPRESENTS THE QUERENT and how they are experiencing the event

2. HIDDEN MOTIVATIONS: What is underlying the mistake?

3. ANCESTRAL/HISTORICAL CONTEXT: What individual and collective past issues are affecting the situation?

4. ENVIRONMENT/OTHERS: How is the querent feeling about and interacting with others?

5. PATH TO SELF FORGIVENESS: How can the querent resolve this mistake internally and begin the process of forgiveness?

6. MAKING REPARATIONS: This position represents the best way to make things right after making a mistake. This card position will usually provide some really practical advice, so look for imagery that demonstrates the best next action to take.

Seven Sisters Spread

```
        ┌─────┐              ┌─────┐
        │     │              │     │
        │     │              │     │
        │  I  │              │  5  │
        └─────┘              └─────┘
   ┌─────┐                   ┌─────┐
   │     │                   │     │
   │     │      ┌─────┐      │     │
   │  2  │      │     │      │  6  │
   └─────┘      │     │      └─────┘
     ┌─────┐    │  4  │      ┌─────┐
     │     │    └─────┘      │     │
     │     │                 │     │
     │  7  │                 │  3  │
     └─────┘                 └─────┘
```

The seven Pleiades were the daughters of the Titan Atlas. Because of their beauty, the hunter Orion lusted after them. At the behest of Artemis, Zeus transformed them into seven stars instead. Even then, Orion, as the constellation Orion, still tracks the Pleiades across the night's sky.

1. Maia: (Eldest solitary sister) How to spend time alone. Self-reflection.

2. Alcyone: (The sister who wards off storms) How to find peace.

3. Celaeno: (The dark sister) An exploration of your shadow self.

4. Electra: (The sister who disappears after grief) How to overcome sadness.

5. Sterope: (The twinkling sister) A creative spark or inspiring message.

6. Taygete: (Companion to Artemis) An exploration of your spirituality.

7. Merope: (The lost sister) Something you need to recover or search for.

Romany Spread

	I	II	III	IV	V	VI	VII

Row A Present

| 1 | 2 | 3 | 4 | 5 | 6 | 7 |

Row B Past

| 8 | 9 | 10 | 11 | 12 | 13 | 14 |

Row C Future

| 15 | 16 | 17 | 18 | 19 | 20 | 21 |

Columns

I: Self

II: Environment

III: Hopes and fears

IV: What the querent expects

V: Hidden factors, unexpected events

VI: Near future (define the time frame before)

VII: Distant future (define the time frame before)

Notes:

Notes:

Notes:

Notes:

Yearly Intentions

MY JOURNEY STARTS TODAY

DECEMBER

JANUARY

FEBRUARY

NOVEMBER

Yearly

MARCH

Outlook

OCTOBER

APRIL

SEPTEMBER

MAY

AUGUST

JUNE

JULY

JANUARY: _____

_____

FEBRUARY:_____

_____

MARCH:_____

_____

APRIL:_____

_____

MAY:_____

_____

JUNE:_____

_____

JULY:_____

_____A

UGUST:_____

_____

SEPTEMBER:_____

_____

OCTOBER:_____

_____

NOVEMBER:_____

_____

DECEMBER:_____

_____

_____

MONTH:_____ FULL MOON: _____ NEW MOON:_____

Sunday	Monday	Tuesday	Wednesday	Thursday	Friday	Saturday

January

Monthly
Energy

Deck used:_____

⬤ New moon
_____
_____

◯ Full moon
_____
_____

| Love | Money | Work | Health | Spirit |

Monthly Energy:_____
_____
_____

Love: _____
_____
_____

Money: _____
_____
_____

Work: _____
_____
_____

Health: _____
_____
_____

Spirit:_____
_____
_____

End of the Month Reflection: _____
_____
_____
_____
_____
_____
_____

New Moon Spread

THIS TIME IS ABOUT NEW BEGINNINGS, PLANTING SEEDS, AND SETTING YOUR INTENTIONS FOR THE LUNAR CYCLE.

1	2	3	4	5

THIS IS A TIME TO MANIFEST YOUR DREAMS!

1. Your energy this month
2. A new opportunity
3. How to make things happen
4. Where I need to grow
5. Guidance from my guides

REFLECTIONS: _____
_____
_____
_____
_____
_____
_____
_____
_____
_____
_____
_____

New Moon Intentions

MANIFEST YOUR DREAMS.

Full Moon Spread

THE FULL MOON IS THE CULMINATION OF OUR INTENTION.
IT IS ABOUT ILLUMINATION AND LETTING GO OF WHAT IS NO LONGER
NEEDED

My favorite spread for a full moon is a variation on what I do daily. I ask a single question, but I use 3 cards to answer it. I find that I get readings with lots of depth and details when I read this way.

RELEASE:
WHAT NO LONGER SERVES ME?

ILLUMINATION:
WHAT HIDDEN THINGS IS THE
MOON REVEALING TO ME?

TRANSFORMATION:
WHAT IS CHANGING?

REFLECTIONS:_ _
_ _
_ _
_ _
_ _
_ _
_ _

Full Moon Intentions

THIS IS A TIME TO CELEBRATE THE CULMINATION OF YOUR INTENTION.

Week of: _____

INTENTION:_____

AFFIRMATION:_____

INTERPRETATION:_____

_____

REFLECTION: _____

DECK USED:

Monday the ___

1._____

_____

2._____

_____

3._____

_____

REFLECTION:_____

DECK USED:

Tuesday the ___

1._____

_____

2._____

_____

3._____

_____

REFLECTION:_____

DECK USED:

Wednesday the ___

1._____

_____

2._____

_____

3._____

_____

REFLECTION:_____

DECK USED:

Thursday the ___

1._____
_____
2._____
_____
3._____
_____

REFLECTION:_____

DECK USED:

Friday the ___

1._____
_____
2._____
_____
3._____
_____

REFLECTION:_____

DECK USED:

Saturday the ___

1._____
_____
2._____
_____
3._____
_____

REFLECTION:_____

DECK USED:

Sunday the ___

1._____
_____
2._____
_____
3._____
_____

REFLECTION:_____

DECK USED:

Week of: _____

INTENTION:_____

AFFIRMATION:_____

INTERPRETATION:_____

_____

REFLECTION: _____

DECK USED:

Monday the ___

1._____

_____

2._____

_____

3._____

_____

REFLECTION:_____

DECK USED:

Tuesday the ___

1._____

_____

2._____

_____

3._____

_____

REFLECTION:_____

DECK USED:

Wednesday the ___

1._____

_____

2._____

_____

3._____

_____

REFLECTION:_____

DECK USED:

Thursday the ___

1._____
_____
2._____
_____
3._____
_____
REFLECTION:_____
DECK USED:

Friday the ___

1._____
_____
2._____
_____
3._____
_____
REFLECTION:_____
DECK USED:

Saturday the ___

1._____
_____
2._____
_____
3._____
_____
REFLECTION:_____
DECK USED:

Sunday the ___

1._____
_____
2._____
_____
3._____
_____
REFLECTION:_____
DECK USED:

Week of: _____

INTENTION:_____

AFFIRMATION:_____

INTERPRETATION:_____

_____

REFLECTION: _____

DECK USED:

Monday the ___

1._____

_____

2._____

_____

3._____

_____

REFLECTION:_____

DECK USED:

Tuesday the ___

1._____

_____

2._____

_____

3._____

_____

REFLECTION:_____

DECK USED:

Wednesday the ___

1._____

_____

2._____

_____

3._____

_____

REFLECTION:_____

DECK USED:

Thursday the ___

1._____
_____
2._____
_____
3._____
_____
REFLECTION:_____

DECK USED:

Friday the ___

1._____
_____
2._____
_____
3._____
_____
REFLECTION:_____

DECK USED:

Saturday the ___

1._____
_____
2._____
_____
3._____
_____
REFLECTION:_____

DECK USED:

Sunday the ___

1._____
_____
2._____
_____
3._____
_____
REFLECTION:_____

DECK USED:

Week of: _____

INTENTION:_____

AFFIRMATION:_____

INTERPRETATION:_____

_____

REFLECTION: _____

DECK USED:

Monday the ___

1._____

_____

2._____

_____

3._____

_____

REFLECTION:_____

DECK USED:

Tuesday the ___

1._____

_____

2._____

_____

3._____

_____

REFLECTION:_____

DECK USED:

Wednesday the ___

1._____

_____

2._____

_____

3._____

_____

REFLECTION:_____

DECK USED:

Thursday the ___

1._____
_____
2._____
_____
3._____
_____
REFLECTION:_____
DECK USED:

Friday the ___

1._____
_____
2._____
_____
3._____
_____
REFLECTION:_____
DECK USED:

Saturday the ___

1._____
_____
2._____
_____
3._____
_____
REFLECTION:_____
DECK USED:

Sunday the ___

1._____
_____
2._____
_____
3._____
_____
REFLECTION:_____
DECK USED:

Week of: _____

INTENTION:_____

AFFIRMATION:_____

INTERPRETATION:_____

_____

REFLECTION: _____

DECK USED:

Monday the ___

1._____

_____

2._____

_____

3._____

_____

REFLECTION:_____

DECK USED:

Tuesday the ___

1._____

_____

2._____

_____

3._____

_____

REFLECTION:_____

DECK USED:

Wednesday the ___

1._____

_____

2._____

_____

3._____

_____

REFLECTION:_____

DECK USED:

Thursday the ___

1._____

_____

2._____

_____

3._____

_____

REFLECTION:_____

DECK USED:

Friday the ___

1._____

_____

2._____

_____

3._____

_____

REFLECTION:_____

DECK USED:

Saturday the ___

1._____

_____

2._____

_____

3._____

_____

REFLECTION:_____

DECK USED:

Sunday the ___

1._____

_____

2._____

_____

3._____

_____

REFLECTION:_____

DECK USED:

MONTH:_____ FULL MOON: _____ NEW MOON:_____

Sunday	Monday	Tuesday	Wednesday	Thursday	Friday	Saturday

February

MONTHLY
ENERGY

DECK USED:_____

● NEW MOON
_____
_____

◐ FULL MOON
_____
_____

LOVE   MONEY   WORK   HEALTH   SPIRIT

MONTHLY ENERGY:_____
_____
_____

LOVE: _____
_____
_____

MONEY: _____
_____
_____

WORK: _____
_____
_____

HEALTH: _____
_____
_____

SPIRIT:_____
_____
_____

END OF THE MONTH REFLECTION: _____
_____
_____
_____
_____
_____
_____

New Moon Spread

THIS TIME IS ABOUT NEW BEGINNINGS, PLANTING SEEDS, AND SETTING YOUR INTENTIONS FOR THE LUNAR CYCLE.

1	2	3	4	5

THIS IS A TIME TO MANIFEST YOUR DREAMS!

1. Your energy this month
2. A new opportunity
3. How to make things happen
4. Where I need to grow
5. Guidance from my guides

REFLECTIONS:_____

_____

_____

_____

_____

_____

_____

_____

_____

_____

_____

_____

New Moon Intentions

MANIFEST YOUR DREAMS.

Full Moon Spread

THE FULL MOON IS THE CULMINATION OF OUR INTENTION. IT IS ABOUT ILLUMINATION AND LETTING GO OF WHAT IS NO LONGER NEEDED

My favorite spread for a full moon is a variation on what I do daily. I ask a single question, but I use 3 cards to answer it. I find that I get readings with lots of depth and details when I read this way.

RELEASE:
WHAT NO LONGER SERVES ME?

ILLUMINATION:
WHAT HIDDEN THINGS IS THE
MOON REVEALING TO ME?

TRANSFORMATION:
WHAT IS CHANGING?

REFLECTIONS:_____
_____
_____
_____
_____
_____
_____
_____

Full Moon Intentions

THIS IS A TIME TO CELEBRATE THE CULMINATION OF YOUR INTENTION.

Week of: _____

INTENTION:_____

AFFIRMATION:_____

INTERPRETATION:_____

_____

REFLECTION: _____

DECK USED:

Monday the ___

1._____

_____

2._____

_____

3._____

_____

REFLECTION:_____

DECK USED:

Tuesday the ___

1._____

_____

2._____

_____

3._____

_____

REFLECTION:_____

DECK USED:

Wednesday the ___

1._____

_____

2._____

_____

3._____

_____

REFLECTION:_____

DECK USED:

Thursday the ___

1._____

_____

2._____

_____

3._____

_____

REFLECTION:_____

DECK USED:

Friday the ___

1._____

_____

2._____

_____

3._____

_____

REFLECTION:_____

DECK USED:

Saturday the ___

1._____

_____

2._____

_____

3._____

_____

REFLECTION:_____

DECK USED:

Sunday the ___

1._____

_____

2._____

_____

3._____

_____

REFLECTION:_____

DECK USED:

Week of: _____

INTENTION:_____

AFFIRMATION:_____

INTERPRETATION:_____
_____

REFLECTION: _____

DECK USED:

Monday the ___

1._____
_____

2._____
_____

3._____
_____

REFLECTION:_____

DECK USED:

Tuesday the ___

1._____
_____

2._____
_____

3._____
_____

REFLECTION:_____

DECK USED:

Wednesday the ___

1._____
_____

2._____
_____

3._____
_____

REFLECTION:_____

DECK USED:

Thursday the ___

1._____
_____
2._____
_____
3._____
_____

REFLECTION:_____

DECK USED:

Friday the ___

1._____
_____
2._____
_____
3._____
_____

REFLECTION:_____

DECK USED:

Saturday the ___

1._____
_____
2._____
_____
3._____
_____

REFLECTION:_____

DECK USED:

Sunday the ___

1._____
_____
2._____
_____
3._____
_____

REFLECTION:_____

DECK USED:

Week of: _____

INTENTION:_____

AFFIRMATION:_____

INTERPRETATION:_____

_____

REFLECTION: _____

DECK USED:

Monday the ___

1._____

_____

2._____

_____

3._____

_____

REFLECTION:_____

DECK USED:

Tuesday the ___

1._____

_____

2._____

_____

3._____

_____

REFLECTION:_____

DECK USED:

Wednesday the ___

1._____

_____

2._____

_____

3._____

_____

REFLECTION:_____

DECK USED:

Thursday the _ _ _

1._____

_____

2._____

_____

3._____

_____

REFLECTION:_____

DECK USED:

Friday the _ _ _

1._____

_____

2._____

_____

3._____

_____

REFLECTION:_____

DECK USED:

Saturday the _ _ _

1._____

_____

2._____

_____

3._____

_____

REFLECTION:_____

DECK USED:

Sunday the _ _ _

1._____

_____

2._____

_____

3._____

_____

REFLECTION:_____

DECK USED:

Week of: _____

INTENTION:_____

AFFIRMATION:_____

INTERPRETATION:_____

_____

REFLECTION: _____

DECK USED:

Monday the ___

1._____

_____

2._____

_____

3._____

_____

REFLECTION:_____

DECK USED:

Tuesday the ___

1._____

_____

2._____

_____

3._____

_____

REFLECTION:_____

DECK USED:

Wednesday the ___

1._____

_____

2._____

_____

3._____

_____

REFLECTION:_____

DECK USED:

Thursday the ___

1._____
   _____
2._____
   _____
3._____
   _____

REFLECTION:_____

DECK USED:

Friday the ___

1._____
   _____
2._____
   _____
3._____
   _____

REFLECTION:_____

DECK USED:

Saturday the ___

1._____
   _____
2._____
   _____
3._____
   _____

REFLECTION:_____

DECK USED:

Sunday the ___

1._____
   _____
2._____
   _____
3._____
   _____

REFLECTION:_____

DECK USED:

Week of: _____

INTENTION:_____

AFFIRMATION:_____

INTERPRETATION:_____

_____

REFLECTION: _____

DECK USED:

Monday the ___

1._____

_____

2._____

_____

3._____

_____

REFLECTION:_____

DECK USED:

Tuesday the ___

1._____

_____

2._____

_____

3._____

_____

REFLECTION:_____

DECK USED:

Wednesday the ___

1._____

_____

2._____

_____

3._____

_____

REFLECTION:_____

DECK USED:

Thursday the ___

1._____
_____
2._____
_____
3._____
_____
REFLECTION:_____
DECK USED:

Friday the ___

1._____
_____
2._____
_____
3._____
_____
REFLECTION:_____
DECK USED:

Saturday the ___

1._____
_____
2._____
_____
3._____
_____
REFLECTION:_____
DECK USED:

Sunday the ___

1._____
_____
2._____
_____
3._____
_____
REFLECTION:_____
DECK USED:

MONTH:_____ FULL MOON: _____ NEW MOON:_____

Sunday	Monday	Tuesday	Wednesday	Thursday	Friday	Saturday

March

MONTHLY ENERGY

DECK USED:_____

● NEW MOON
_____
_____

◐ FULL MOON
_____
_____

LOVE MONEY WORK HEALTH SPIRIT

MONTHLY ENERGY:_____
_____
_____

LOVE: _____
_____
_____

MONEY: _____
_____
_____

WORK: _____
_____
_____

HEALTH: _____
_____
_____

SPIRIT:_____
_____
_____

END OF THE MONTH REFLECTION: _____
_____
_____
_____
_____
_____
_____

New Moon Spread

THIS TIME IS ABOUT NEW BEGINNINGS, PLANTING SEEDS, AND SETTING YOUR INTENTIONS FOR THE LUNAR CYCLE.

1	2	3	4	5

THIS IS A TIME TO MANIFEST YOUR DREAMS!

1. Your energy this month
2. A new opportunity
3. How to make things happen
4. Where I need to grow
5. Guidance from my guides

REFLECTIONS:_____

_____

_____

_____

_____

_____

_____

_____

_____

_____

_____

New Moon Intentions

MANIFEST YOUR DREAMS.

Full Moon Spread

THE FULL MOON IS THE CULMINATION OF OUR INTENTION. IT IS ABOUT ILLUMINATION AND LETTING GO OF WHAT IS NO LONGER NEEDED

My favorite spread for a full moon is a variation on what I do daily. I ask a single question, but I use 3 cards to answer it. I find that I get readings with lots of depth and details when I read this way.

RELEASE:
WHAT NO LONGER SERVES ME?

ILLUMINATION:
WHAT HIDDEN THINGS IS THE
MOON REVEALING TO ME?

TRANSFORMATION:
WHAT IS CHANGING?

REFLECTIONS:_ _
_ _
_ _
_ _
_ _
_ _
_ _
_ _

Full Moon Intentions

THIS IS A TIME TO CELEBRATE THE CULMINATION OF YOUR INTENTION.

Week of: _____

INTENTION:_____

AFFIRMATION:_____

INTERPRETATION:_____

_____

REFLECTION: _____

DECK USED:

Monday the ___

1._____

_____

2._____

_____

3._____

_____

REFLECTION:_____

DECK USED:

Tuesday the ___

1._____

_____

2._____

_____

3._____

_____

REFLECTION:_____

DECK USED:

Wednesday the ___

1._____

_____

2._____

_____

3._____

_____

REFLECTION:_____

DECK USED:

Thursday the ___

1._____
_____
2._____
_____
3._____
_____

REFLECTION:_____

DECK USED:

Friday the ___

1._____
_____
2._____
_____
3._____
_____

REFLECTION:_____

DECK USED:

Saturday the ___

1._____
_____
2._____
_____
3._____
_____

REFLECTION:_____

DECK USED:

Sunday the ___

1._____
_____
2._____
_____
3._____
_____

REFLECTION:_____

DECK USED:

Week of: _____

INTENTION:_____

AFFIRMATION:_____

INTERPRETATION:_____

_____

REFLECTION: _____

DECK USED:

Monday the _ _ _

1._____

_____

2._____

_____

3._____

_____

REFLECTION:_____

DECK USED:

Tuesday the _ _ _

1._____

_____

2._____

_____

3._____

_____

REFLECTION:_____

DECK USED:

Wednesday the _ _ _

1._____

_____

2._____

_____

3._____

_____

REFLECTION:_____

DECK USED:

Thursday the ___

1._____
_____
2._____
_____
3._____
_____

REFLECTION:_____

DECK USED:

Friday the ___

1._____
_____
2._____
_____
3._____
_____

REFLECTION:_____

DECK USED:

Saturday the ___

1._____
_____
2._____
_____
3._____
_____

REFLECTION:_____

DECK USED:

Sunday the ___

1._____
_____
2._____
_____
3._____
_____

REFLECTION:_____

DECK USED:

Week of: _____

INTENTION:_____

AFFIRMATION:_____

INTERPRETATION:_____

_____

REFLECTION: _____

DECK USED:

Monday the ___

1._____

_____

2._____

_____

3._____

_____

REFLECTION:_____

DECK USED:

Tuesday the ___

1._____

_____

2._____

_____

3._____

_____

REFLECTION:_____

DECK USED:

Wednesday the ___

1._____

_____

2._____

_____

3._____

_____

REFLECTION:_____

DECK USED:

Thursday the ___

1._____
_____
2._____
_____
3._____
_____
REFLECTION:_____
DECK USED:

Friday the ___

1._____
_____
2._____
_____
3._____
_____
REFLECTION:_____
DECK USED:

Saturday the ___

1._____
_____
2._____
_____
3._____
_____
REFLECTION:_____
DECK USED:

Sunday the ___

1._____
_____
2._____
_____
3._____
_____
REFLECTION:_____
DECK USED:

Week of: _____

INTENTION:_____

AFFIRMATION:_____

INTERPRETATION:_____

_____

REFLECTION: _____

DECK USED:

Monday the ___

1._____

_____

2._____

_____

3._____

_____

REFLECTION:_____

DECK USED:

Tuesday the ___

1._____

_____

2._____

_____

3._____

_____

REFLECTION:_____

DECK USED:

Wednesday the ___

1._____

_____

2._____

_____

3._____

_____

REFLECTION:_____

DECK USED:

Thursday the ___

1._____
_____
2._____
_____
3._____
_____
REFLECTION:_____
DECK USED:

Friday the ___

1._____
_____
2._____
_____
3._____
_____
REFLECTION:_____
DECK USED:

Saturday the ___

1._____
_____
2._____
_____
3._____
_____
REFLECTION:_____
DECK USED:

Sunday the ___

1._____
_____
2._____
_____
3._____
_____
REFLECTION:_____
DECK USED:

Week of: _____

INTENTION:_____

AFFIRMATION:_____

INTERPRETATION:_____

_____

REFLECTION: _____

DECK USED:

Monday the ___

1._____

_____

2._____

_____

3._____

_____

REFLECTION:_____

DECK USED:

Tuesday the ___

1._____

_____

2._____

_____

3._____

_____

REFLECTION:_____

DECK USED:

Wednesday the ___

1._____

_____

2._____

_____

3._____

_____

REFLECTION:_____

DECK USED:

Thursday the ___

1._____
_____
2._____
_____
3._____
_____
REFLECTION:_____
DECK USED:

Friday the ___

1._____
_____
2._____
_____
3._____
_____
REFLECTION:_____
DECK USED:

Saturday the ___

1._____
_____
2._____
_____
3._____
_____
REFLECTION:_____
DECK USED:

Sunday the ___

1._____
_____
2._____
_____
3._____
_____
REFLECTION:_____
DECK USED:

| MONTH:_____ | FULL MOON: _____ | NEW MOON:_____ |

Sunday	Monday	Tuesday	Wednesday	Thursday	Friday	Saturday

April

MONTHLY
ENERGY

DECK USED:_____

NEW MOON
_____
_____

FULL MOON
_____
_____

LOVE   MONEY   WORK   HEALTH   SPIRIT

MONTHLY ENERGY:_____
_____
_____

LOVE: _____
_____
_____

MONEY: _____
_____
_____

WORK: _____
_____
_____

HEALTH: _____
_____
_____

SPIRIT:_____
_____
_____

END OF THE MONTH REFLECTION: _____
_____
_____
_____
_____
_____
_____

New Moon Spread

THIS TIME IS ABOUT NEW BEGINNINGS, PLANTING SEEDS, AND SETTING YOUR INTENTIONS FOR THE LUNAR CYCLE.

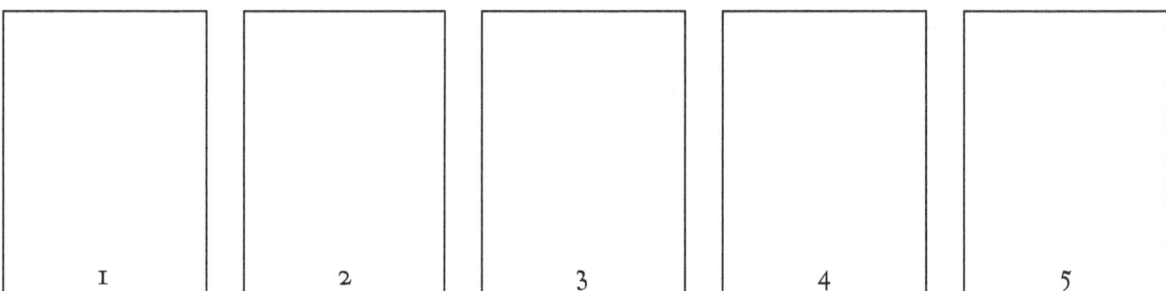

1   2   3   4   5

THIS IS A TIME TO MANIFEST YOUR DREAMS!

1. Your energy this month
2. A new opportunity
3. How to make things happen
4. Where I need to grow
5. Guidance from my guides

REFLECTIONS:_____

_____

_____

_____

_____

_____

_____

_____

_____

_____

_____

New Moon Intentions

MANIFEST YOUR DREAMS.

Full Moon Spread

THE FULL MOON IS THE CULMINATION OF OUR INTENTION.
IT IS ABOUT ILLUMINATION AND LETTING GO OF WHAT IS NO LONGER NEEDED

My favorite spread for a full moon is a variation on what I do daily. I ask a single question, but I use 3 cards to answer it. I find that I get readings with lots of depth and details when I read this way.

RELEASE:
WHAT NO LONGER SERVES ME?

ILLUMINATION:
WHAT HIDDEN THINGS IS THE
MOON REVEALING TO ME?

TRANSFORMATION:
WHAT IS CHANGING?

REFLECTIONS:_____

_____

_____

_____

_____

_____

_____

_____

Full Moon Intentions

THIS IS A TIME TO CELEBRATE THE CULMINATION OF YOUR INTENTION.

Week of: _____

INTENTION:_____

AFFIRMATION:_____

INTERPRETATION:_____

_____

REFLECTION: _____

DECK USED:

Monday the ___

1._____

_____

2._____

_____

3._____

_____

REFLECTION:_____

DECK USED:

Tuesday the ___

1._____

_____

2._____

_____

3._____

_____

REFLECTION:_____

DECK USED:

Wednesday the ___

1._____

_____

2._____

_____

3._____

_____

REFLECTION:_____

DECK USED:

Thursday the ___

1._____
_____
2._____
_____
3._____
_____
REFLECTION:_____
DECK USED:

Friday the ___

1._____
_____
2._____
_____
3._____
_____
REFLECTION:_____
DECK USED:

Saturday the ___

1._____
_____
2._____
_____
3._____
_____
REFLECTION:_____
DECK USED:

Sunday the ___

1._____
_____
2._____
_____
3._____
_____
REFLECTION:_____
DECK USED:

Week of: _____

INTENTION:_____

AFFIRMATION:_____

INTERPRETATION:_____

_____

REFLECTION: _____

DECK USED:

Monday the ___

1._____

_____

2._____

_____

3._____

_____

REFLECTION:_____

DECK USED:

Tuesday the ___

1._____

_____

2._____

_____

3._____

_____

REFLECTION:_____

DECK USED:

Wednesday the ___

1._____

_____

2._____

_____

3._____

_____

REFLECTION:_____

DECK USED:

Thursday the ___

1._____

_____

2._____

_____

3._____

_____

REFLECTION:_____

DECK USED:

Friday the ___

1._____

_____

2._____

_____

3._____

_____

REFLECTION:_____

DECK USED:

Saturday the ___

1._____

_____

2._____

_____

3._____

_____

REFLECTION:_____

DECK USED:

Sunday the ___

1._____

_____

2._____

_____

3._____

_____

REFLECTION:_____

DECK USED:

Week of: _____

INTENTION:_____

AFFIRMATION:_____

INTERPRETATION:_____

_____

REFLECTION: _____

DECK USED:

Monday the ___

1._____

_____

2._____

_____

3._____

_____

REFLECTION:_____

DECK USED:

Tuesday the ___

1._____

_____

2._____

_____

3._____

_____

REFLECTION:_____

DECK USED:

Wednesday the ___

1._____

_____

2._____

_____

3._____

_____

REFLECTION:_____

DECK USED:

Thursday the ___

1._____

_____

2._____

_____

3._____

_____

REFLECTION:_____

DECK USED:

Friday the ___

1._____

_____

2._____

_____

3._____

_____

REFLECTION:_____

DECK USED:

Saturday the ___

1._____

_____

2._____

_____

3._____

_____

REFLECTION:_____

DECK USED:

Sunday the ___

1._____

_____

2._____

_____

3._____

_____

REFLECTION:_____

DECK USED:

Week of: _____

INTENTION:_____

AFFIRMATION:_____

INTERPRETATION:_____

_____

REFLECTION: _____

DECK USED:

Monday the ___

1._____

_____

2._____

_____

3._____

_____

REFLECTION:_____

DECK USED:

Tuesday the ___

1._____

_____

2._____

_____

3._____

_____

REFLECTION:_____

DECK USED:

Wednesday the ___

1._____

_____

2._____

_____

3._____

_____

REFLECTION:_____

DECK USED:

Thursday the ___

1._____
_____
2._____
_____
3._____
_____
REFLECTION:_____
DECK USED:

Friday the ___

1._____
_____
2._____
_____
3._____
_____
REFLECTION:_____
DECK USED:

Saturday the ___

1._____
_____
2._____
_____
3._____
_____
REFLECTION:_____
DECK USED:

Sunday the ___

1._____
_____
2._____
_____
3._____
_____
REFLECTION:_____
DECK USED:

	Week of: _____
	INTENTION:_____
	AFFIRMATION:_____

INTERPRETATION:_____

_____

REFLECTION: _____

DECK USED:

Monday the ___

	1._____
	_____
	2._____
	_____
	3._____
	_____
	REFLECTION:_____
	DECK USED:

Tuesday the ___

	1._____
	_____
	2._____
	_____
	3._____
	_____
	REFLECTION:_____
	DECK USED:

Wednesday the ___

	1._____
	_____
	2._____
	_____
	3._____
	_____
	REFLECTION:_____
	DECK USED:

Thursday the ___

1._____
_____

2._____
_____

3._____
_____

REFLECTION:_____

DECK USED:

Friday the ___

1._____
_____

2._____
_____

3._____
_____

REFLECTION:_____

DECK USED:

Saturday the ___

1._____
_____

2._____
_____

3._____
_____

REFLECTION:_____

DECK USED:

Sunday the ___

1._____
_____

2._____
_____

3._____
_____

REFLECTION:_____

DECK USED:

MONTH:_____ FULL MOON: _____ NEW MOON:_____

Sunday	Monday	Tuesday	Wednesday	Thursday	Friday	Saturday

May

[ ] MONTHLY ENERGY

DECK USED:_____

● NEW MOON
_____
_____

◐ FULL MOON
_____
_____

[ ] LOVE   [ ] MONEY   [ ] WORK   [ ] HEALTH   [ ] SPIRIT

MONTHLY ENERGY:_____
_____
_____

LOVE: _____
_____
_____

MONEY: _____
_____
_____

WORK: _____
_____
_____

HEALTH: _____
_____
_____

SPIRIT:_____
_____
_____

END OF THE MONTH REFLECTION: _____
_____
_____
_____
_____
_____
_____

New Moon Spread

THIS TIME IS ABOUT NEW BEGINNINGS, PLANTING SEEDS, AND SETTING YOUR INTENTIONS FOR THE LUNAR CYCLE.

1	2	3	4	5

THIS IS A TIME TO MANIFEST YOUR DREAMS!

1. Your energy this month
2. A new opportunity
3. How to make things happen
4. Where I need to grow
5. Guidance from my guides

REFLECTIONS:_____
_____
_____
_____
_____
_____
_____
_____
_____
_____
_____
_____

New Moon Intentions

MANIFEST YOUR DREAMS.

Full Moon Spread

THE FULL MOON IS THE CULMINATION OF OUR INTENTION.
IT IS ABOUT ILLUMINATION AND LETTING GO OF WHAT IS NO LONGER NEEDED

My favorite spread for a full moon is a variation on what I do daily. I ask a single question, but I use 3 cards to answer it. I find that I get readings with lots of depth and details when I read this way.

RELEASE:
WHAT NO LONGER SERVES ME?

ILLUMINATION:
WHAT HIDDEN THINGS IS THE
MOON REVEALING TO ME?

TRANSFORMATION:
WHAT IS CHANGING?

REFLECTIONS:_____
_____
_____
_____
_____
_____
_____
_____

Full Moon Intentions

THIS IS A TIME TO CELEBRATE THE CULMINATION OF YOUR INTENTION.

Week of: _____

INTENTION:_____

AFFIRMATION:_____

INTERPRETATION:_____

_____

REFLECTION: _____

DECK USED:

Monday the ___

1._____

_____

2._____

_____

3._____

_____

REFLECTION:_____

DECK USED:

Tuesday the ___

1._____

_____

2._____

_____

3._____

_____

REFLECTION:_____

DECK USED:

Wednesday the ___

1._____

_____

2._____

_____

3._____

_____

REFLECTION:_____

DECK USED:

Thursday the ___

1._____
_____
2._____
_____
3._____
_____
REFLECTION:_____
DECK USED:

Friday the ___

1._____
_____
2._____
_____
3._____
_____
REFLECTION:_____
DECK USED:

Saturday the ___

1._____
_____
2._____
_____
3._____
_____
REFLECTION:_____
DECK USED:

Sunday the ___

1._____
_____
2._____
_____
3._____
_____
REFLECTION:_____
DECK USED:

Week of: _____

INTENTION:_____

AFFIRMATION:_____

INTERPRETATION:_____

_____

REFLECTION: _____

DECK USED:

Monday the ___

1._____

_____

2._____

_____

3._____

_____

REFLECTION:_____

DECK USED:

Tuesday the ___

1._____

_____

2._____

_____

3._____

_____

REFLECTION:_____

DECK USED:

Wednesday the ___

1._____

_____

2._____

_____

3._____

_____

REFLECTION:_____

DECK USED:

Thursday the ___

1. _____
_____
2. _____
_____
3. _____
_____

REFLECTION:_____

DECK USED:

Friday the ___

1. _____
_____
2. _____
_____
3. _____
_____

REFLECTION:_____

DECK USED:

Saturday the ___

1. _____
_____
2. _____
_____
3. _____
_____

REFLECTION:_____

DECK USED:

Sunday the ___

1. _____
_____
2. _____
_____
3. _____
_____

REFLECTION:_____

DECK USED:

Week of: _____

INTENTION:_____

AFFIRMATION:_____

INTERPRETATION:_____

_____

REFLECTION: _____

DECK USED:

Monday the ___

1._____

_____

2._____

_____

3._____

_____

REFLECTION:_____

DECK USED:

Tuesday the ___

1._____

_____

2._____

_____

3._____

_____

REFLECTION:_____

DECK USED:

Wednesday the ___

1._____

_____

2._____

_____

3._____

_____

REFLECTION:_____

DECK USED:

Thursday the ___

1._____
_____
2._____
_____
3._____
_____

REFLECTION:_____

DECK USED:

Friday the ___

1._____
_____
2._____
_____
3._____
_____

REFLECTION:_____

DECK USED:

Saturday the ___

1._____
_____
2._____
_____
3._____
_____

REFLECTION:_____

DECK USED:

Sunday the ___

1._____
_____
2._____
_____
3._____
_____

REFLECTION:_____

DECK USED:

Week of: _____

INTENTION:_____

AFFIRMATION:_____

INTERPRETATION:_____

_____

REFLECTION: _____

DECK USED:

Monday the ___

1._____

_____

2._____

_____

3._____

_____

REFLECTION:_____

DECK USED:

Tuesday the ___

1._____

_____

2._____

_____

3._____

_____

REFLECTION:_____

DECK USED:

Wednesday the ___

1._____

_____

2._____

_____

3._____

_____

REFLECTION:_____

DECK USED:

Thursday the ___

1._____
_____
2._____
_____
3._____
_____

REFLECTION:_____

DECK USED:

Friday the ___

1._____
_____
2._____
_____
3._____
_____

REFLECTION:_____

DECK USED:

Saturday the ___

1._____
_____
2._____
_____
3._____
_____

REFLECTION:_____

DECK USED:

Sunday the ___

1._____
_____
2._____
_____
3._____
_____

REFLECTION:_____

DECK USED:

Week of: _____

INTENTION:_____

AFFIRMATION:_____

INTERPRETATION:_____

_____

REFLECTION: _____

DECK USED:

Monday the ___

1._____

_____

2._____

_____

3._____

_____

REFLECTION:_____

DECK USED:

Tuesday the ___

1._____

_____

2._____

_____

3._____

_____

REFLECTION:_____

DECK USED:

Wednesday the ___

1._____

_____

2._____

_____

3._____

_____

REFLECTION:_____

DECK USED:

Thursday the ___

1._____
_____
2._____
_____
3._____
_____
REFLECTION:_____
DECK USED:

Friday the ___

1._____
_____
2._____
_____
3._____
_____
REFLECTION:_____
DECK USED:

Saturday the ___

1._____
_____
2._____
_____
3._____
_____
REFLECTION:_____
DECK USED:

Sunday the ___

1._____
_____
2._____
_____
3._____
_____
REFLECTION:_____
DECK USED:

MONTH:_____ FULL MOON: _____ NEW MOON:_____

Sunday	Monday	Tuesday	Wednesday	Thursday	Friday	Saturday

June

DECK USED:_____

NEW MOON
_____
_____

FULL MOON
_____
_____

[ ] LOVE [ ] MONEY [ ] WORK [ ] HEALTH [ ] SPIRIT

MONTHLY ENERGY:_____
_____
_____

LOVE: _____
_____
_____

MONEY: _____
_____
_____

WORK: _____
_____
_____

HEALTH: _____
_____
_____

SPIRIT:_____
_____
_____

END OF THE MONTH REFLECTION: _____
_____
_____
_____
_____

New Moon Spread

THIS TIME IS ABOUT NEW BEGINNINGS, PLANTING SEEDS, AND SETTING YOUR INTENTIONS FOR THE LUNAR CYCLE.

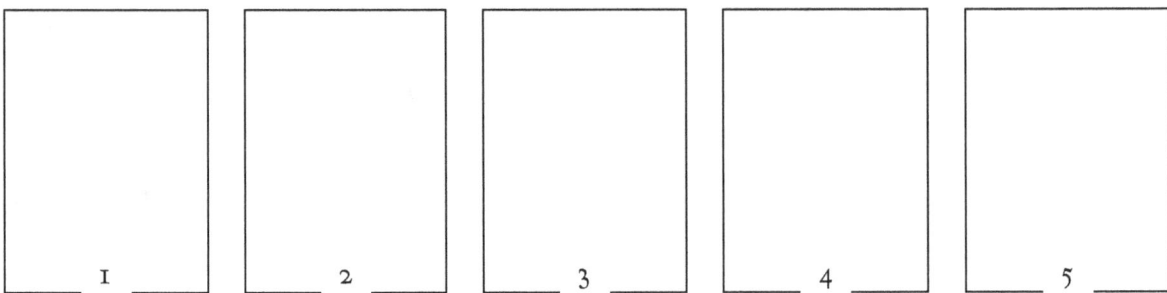

| 1 | 2 | 3 | 4 | 5 |

THIS IS A TIME TO MANIFEST YOUR DREAMS!

1. Your energy this month
2. A new opportunity
3. How to make things happen
4. Where I need to grow
5. Guidance from my guides

REFLECTIONS:_____
_____
_____
_____
_____
_____
_____
_____
_____
_____
_____

New Moon Intentions

MANIFEST YOUR DREAMS.

Full Moon Spread

THE FULL MOON IS THE CULMINATION OF OUR INTENTION.
IT IS ABOUT ILLUMINATION AND LETTING GO OF WHAT IS NO LONGER NEEDED

My favorite spread for a full moon is a variation on what I do daily. I ask a single question, but I use 3 cards to answer it. I find that I get readings with lots of depth and details when I read this way.

RELEASE:
WHAT NO LONGER SERVES ME?

ILLUMINATION:
WHAT HIDDEN THINGS IS THE
MOON REVEALING TO ME?

TRANSFORMATION:
WHAT IS CHANGING?

REFLECTIONS:_____

_____

_____

_____

_____

_____

_____

_____

Full Moon Intentions

THIS IS A TIME TO CELEBRATE THE CULMINATION OF YOUR INTENTION.

Week of: _____

INTENTION:_____

AFFIRMATION:_____

INTERPRETATION:_____

_____

REFLECTION: _____

DECK USED:

Monday the ___

1._____

_____

2._____

_____

3._____

_____

REFLECTION:_____

DECK USED:

Tuesday the ___

1._____

_____

2._____

_____

3._____

_____

REFLECTION:_____

DECK USED:

Wednesday the ___

1._____

_____

2._____

_____

3._____

_____

REFLECTION:_____

DECK USED:

Thursday the ___

1._____

_____

2._____

_____

3._____

_____

REFLECTION:_____

DECK USED:

Friday the ___

1._____

_____

2._____

_____

3._____

_____

REFLECTION:_____

DECK USED:

Saturday the ___

1._____

_____

2._____

_____

3._____

_____

REFLECTION:_____

DECK USED:

Sunday the ___

1._____

_____

2._____

_____

3._____

_____

REFLECTION:_____

DECK USED:

Week of: _____

INTENTION:_____

AFFIRMATION:_____

INTERPRETATION:_____

_____

REFLECTION: _____

DECK USED:

Monday the ___

1._____

_____

2._____

_____

3._____

_____

REFLECTION:_____

DECK USED:

Tuesday the ___

1._____

_____

2._____

_____

3._____

_____

REFLECTION:_____

DECK USED:

Wednesday the ___

1._____

_____

2._____

_____

3._____

_____

REFLECTION:_____

DECK USED:

Thursday the ___

1._____
_____
2._____
_____
3._____
_____
REFLECTION:_____
DECK USED:

Friday the ___

1._____
_____
2._____
_____
3._____
_____
REFLECTION:_____
DECK USED:

Saturday the ___

1._____
_____
2._____
_____
3._____
_____
REFLECTION:_____
DECK USED:

Sunday the ___

1._____
_____
2._____
_____
3._____
_____
REFLECTION:_____
DECK USED:

	Week of: _____
	INTENTION:_____
	AFFIRMATION:_____

INTERPRETATION:_____

_____

REFLECTION: _____

DECK USED:

Monday the ___

1._____

_____

2._____

_____

3._____

_____

REFLECTION:_____

DECK USED:

Tuesday the ___

1._____

_____

2._____

_____

3._____

_____

REFLECTION:_____

DECK USED:

Wednesday the ___

1._____

_____

2._____

_____

3._____

_____

REFLECTION:_____

DECK USED:

Thursday the ___

1._____

_____

2._____

_____

3._____

_____

REFLECTION:_____

DECK USED:

Friday the ___

1._____

_____

2._____

_____

3._____

_____

REFLECTION:_____

DECK USED:

Saturday the ___

1._____

_____

2._____

_____

3._____

_____

REFLECTION:_____

DECK USED:

Sunday the ___

1._____

_____

2._____

_____

3._____

_____

REFLECTION:_____

DECK USED:

	Week of: _____
	INTENTION:_____
	AFFIRMATION:_____

INTERPRETATION:_____

_____

REFLECTION: _____

DECK USED:

Monday the ___

1._____

_____

2._____

_____

3._____

_____

REFLECTION:_____

DECK USED:

Tuesday the ___

1._____

_____

2._____

_____

3._____

_____

REFLECTION:_____

DECK USED:

Wednesday the ___

1._____

_____

2._____

_____

3._____

_____

REFLECTION:_____

DECK USED:

Thursday the ___

1._____
_____
2._____
_____
3._____
_____

REFLECTION:_____

DECK USED:

Friday the ___

1._____
_____
2._____
_____
3._____
_____

REFLECTION:_____

DECK USED:

Saturday the ___

1._____
_____
2._____
_____
3._____
_____

REFLECTION:_____

DECK USED:

Sunday the ___

1._____
_____
2._____
_____
3._____
_____

REFLECTION:_____

DECK USED:

Week of: _____

INTENTION:_____

AFFIRMATION:_____

INTERPRETATION:_____

_____

REFLECTION: _____

DECK USED:

Monday the ___

1._____

_____

2._____

_____

3._____

_____

REFLECTION:_____

DECK USED:

Tuesday the ___

1._____

_____

2._____

_____

3._____

_____

REFLECTION:_____

DECK USED:

Wednesday the ___

1._____

_____

2._____

_____

3._____

_____

REFLECTION:_____

DECK USED:

Thursday the ___

1._____
_____
2._____
_____
3._____
_____

REFLECTION:_____

DECK USED:

Friday the ___

1._____
_____
2._____
_____
3._____
_____

REFLECTION:_____

DECK USED:

Saturday the ___

1._____
_____
2._____
_____
3._____
_____

REFLECTION:_____

DECK USED:

Sunday the ___

1._____
_____
2._____
_____
3._____
_____

REFLECTION:_____

DECK USED:

MONTH:_____ FULL MOON: _____ NEW MOON:_____

Sunday	Monday	Tuesday	Wednesday	Thursday	Friday	Saturday

July

MONTHLY ENERGY

DECK USED:_____

NEW MOON
_____
_____

FULL MOON
_____
_____

LOVE   MONEY   WORK   HEALTH   SPIRIT

MONTHLY ENERGY:_____
_____
_____

LOVE: _____
_____
_____

MONEY: _____
_____
_____

WORK: _____
_____
_____

HEALTH: _____
_____
_____

SPIRIT:_____
_____
_____

END OF THE MONTH REFLECTION: _____
_____
_____
_____
_____
_____

New Moon Spread

THIS TIME IS ABOUT NEW BEGINNINGS, PLANTING SEEDS, AND SETTING YOUR INTENTIONS FOR THE LUNAR CYCLE.

1	2	3	4	5

THIS IS A TIME TO MANIFEST YOUR DREAMS!

1. Your energy this month
2. A new opportunity
3. How to make things happen
4. Where I need to grow
5. Guidance from my guides

REFLECTIONS: _____

_____

_____

_____

_____

_____

_____

_____

_____

_____

_____

New Moon Intentions

MANIFEST YOUR DREAMS.

Full Moon Spread

THE FULL MOON IS THE CULMINATION OF OUR INTENTION.
IT IS ABOUT ILLUMINATION AND LETTING GO OF WHAT IS NO LONGER NEEDED

My favorite spread for a full moon is a variation on what I do daily. I ask a single question, but I use 3 cards to answer it. I find that I get readings with lots of depth and details when I read this way.

RELEASE:
WHAT NO LONGER SERVES ME?

ILLUMINATION:
WHAT HIDDEN THINGS IS THE
MOON REVEALING TO ME?

TRANSFORMATION:
WHAT IS CHANGING?

REFLECTIONS:_____

_____

_____

_____

_____

_____

_____

_____

Full Moon Intentions

THIS IS A TIME TO CELEBRATE THE CULMINATION OF YOUR INTENTION.

Week of: _____

INTENTION:_____

AFFIRMATION:_____

INTERPRETATION:_____

_____

REFLECTION: _____

DECK USED:

Monday the ___

1._____

_____

2._____

_____

3._____

_____

REFLECTION:_____

DECK USED:

Tuesday the ___

1._____

_____

2._____

_____

3._____

_____

REFLECTION:_____

DECK USED:

Wednesday the ___

1._____

_____

2._____

_____

3._____

_____

REFLECTION:_____

DECK USED:

Thursday the ___

1._____
_____
2._____
_____
3._____
_____
REFLECTION:_____

DECK USED:

Friday the ___

1._____
_____
2._____
_____
3._____
_____
REFLECTION:_____

DECK USED:

Saturday the ___

1._____
_____
2._____
_____
3._____
_____
REFLECTION:_____

DECK USED:

Sunday the ___

1._____
_____
2._____
_____
3._____
_____
REFLECTION:_____

DECK USED:

Week of: _____

INTENTION:_____

AFFIRMATION:_____

INTERPRETATION:_____

_____

REFLECTION: _____

DECK USED:

Monday the ___

1._____

_____

2._____

_____

3._____

_____

REFLECTION:_____

DECK USED:

Tuesday the ___

1._____

_____

2._____

_____

3._____

_____

REFLECTION:_____

DECK USED:

Wednesday the ___

1._____

_____

2._____

_____

3._____

_____

REFLECTION:_____

DECK USED:

Thursday the ___

1._____
_____
2._____
_____
3._____
_____

REFLECTION:_____

DECK USED:

Friday the ___

1._____
_____
2._____
_____
3._____
_____

REFLECTION:_____

DECK USED:

Saturday the ___

1._____
_____
2._____
_____
3._____
_____

REFLECTION:_____

DECK USED:

Sunday the ___

1._____
_____
2._____
_____
3._____
_____

REFLECTION:_____

DECK USED:

	Week of: _____
	INTENTION:_____
	AFFIRMATION:_____
INTERPRETATION:_____
_____
REFLECTION: _____
DECK USED:

Monday the ___

1._____
_____
2._____
_____
3._____
_____
REFLECTION:_____
DECK USED:

Tuesday the ___

1._____
_____
2._____
_____
3._____
_____
REFLECTION:_____
DECK USED:

Wednesday the ___

1._____
_____
2._____
_____
3._____
_____
REFLECTION:_____
DECK USED:

Thursday the ___

1._____
_____
2._____
_____
3._____
_____

REFLECTION:_____

DECK USED:

Friday the ___

1._____
_____
2._____
_____
3._____
_____

REFLECTION:_____

DECK USED:

Saturday the ___

1._____
_____
2._____
_____
3._____
_____

REFLECTION:_____

DECK USED:

Sunday the ___

1._____
_____
2._____
_____
3._____
_____

REFLECTION:_____

DECK USED:

Week of: _____

INTENTION:_____

AFFIRMATION:_____

INTERPRETATION:_____

_____

REFLECTION: _____

DECK USED:

Monday the ___

1._____

_____

2._____

_____

3._____

_____

REFLECTION:_____

DECK USED:

Tuesday the ___

1._____

_____

2._____

_____

3._____

_____

REFLECTION:_____

DECK USED:

Wednesday the ___

1._____

_____

2._____

_____

3._____

_____

REFLECTION:_____

DECK USED:

Thursday the ___

1._____
_____
2._____
_____
3._____
_____

REFLECTION:_____

DECK USED:

Friday the ___

1._____
_____
2._____
_____
3._____
_____

REFLECTION:_____

DECK USED:

Saturday the ___

1._____
_____
2._____
_____
3._____
_____

REFLECTION:_____

DECK USED:

Sunday the ___

1._____
_____
2._____
_____
3._____
_____

REFLECTION:_____

DECK USED:

Week of: _____

INTENTION:_____

AFFIRMATION:_____

INTERPRETATION:_____

_____

REFLECTION: _____

DECK USED:

Monday the ___

1._____

_____

2._____

_____

3._____

_____

REFLECTION:_____

DECK USED:

Tuesday the ___

1._____

_____

2._____

_____

3._____

_____

REFLECTION:_____

DECK USED:

Wednesday the ___

1._____

_____

2._____

_____

3._____

_____

REFLECTION:_____

DECK USED:

Thursday the ___

1._____
_____
2._____
_____
3._____
_____
REFLECTION:_____
DECK USED:

Friday the ___

1._____
_____
2._____
_____
3._____
_____
REFLECTION:_____
DECK USED:

Saturday the ___

1._____
_____
2._____
_____
3._____
_____
REFLECTION:_____
DECK USED:

Sunday the ___

1._____
_____
2._____
_____
3._____
_____
REFLECTION:_____
DECK USED:

MONTH:_____ FULL MOON: _____ NEW MOON:_____

Sunday	Monday	Tuesday	Wednesday	Thursday	Friday	Saturday

August

MONTHLY ENERGY

DECK USED: _____

NEW MOON
_____
_____

FULL MOON
_____
_____

LOVE | MONEY | WORK | HEALTH | SPIRIT

MONTHLY ENERGY: _____
_____
_____

LOVE: _____
_____
_____

MONEY: _____
_____
_____

WORK: _____
_____
_____

HEALTH: _____
_____
_____

SPIRIT: _____
_____
_____

END OF THE MONTH REFLECTION: _____
_____
_____
_____
_____
_____
_____

New Moon Spread

THIS TIME IS ABOUT NEW BEGINNINGS, PLANTING SEEDS, AND SETTING YOUR INTENTIONS FOR THE LUNAR CYCLE.

1	2	3	4	5

THIS IS A TIME TO MANIFEST YOUR DREAMS!

1. Your energy this month
2. A new opportunity
3. How to make things happen
4. Where I need to grow
5. Guidance from my guides

REFLECTIONS:_____
_____
_____
_____
_____
_____
_____
_____
_____
_____
_____

New Moon Intentions

MANIFEST YOUR DREAMS.

Full Moon Spread

THE FULL MOON IS THE CULMINATION OF OUR INTENTION.
IT IS ABOUT ILLUMINATION AND LETTING GO OF WHAT IS NO LONGER
NEEDED

My favorite spread for a full moon is a variation on what I do daily. I ask a single question, but I use 3 cards to answer it. I find that I get readings with lots of depth and details when I read this way.

RELEASE:
WHAT NO LONGER SERVES ME?

ILLUMINATION:
WHAT HIDDEN THINGS IS THE
MOON REVEALING TO ME?

TRANSFORMATION:
WHAT IS CHANGING?

REFLECTIONS:_____

_____

_____

_____

_____

_____

_____

_____

Full Moon Intentions

THIS IS A TIME TO CELEBRATE THE CULMINATION OF YOUR INTENTION.

Week of: _____

INTENTION:_____

AFFIRMATION:_____

INTERPRETATION:_____

_____

REFLECTION: _____

DECK USED:

Monday the ___

1._____

_____

2._____

_____

3._____

_____

REFLECTION:_____

DECK USED:

Tuesday the ___

1._____

_____

2._____

_____

3._____

_____

REFLECTION:_____

DECK USED:

Wednesday the ___

1._____

_____

2._____

_____

3._____

_____

REFLECTION:_____

DECK USED:

Thursday the ___

1._____

_____

2._____

_____

3._____

_____

REFLECTION:_____

DECK USED:

Friday the ___

1._____

_____

2._____

_____

3._____

_____

REFLECTION:_____

DECK USED:

Saturday the ___

1._____

_____

2._____

_____

3._____

_____

REFLECTION:_____

DECK USED:

Sunday the ___

1._____

_____

2._____

_____

3._____

_____

REFLECTION:_____

DECK USED:

Week of: _____

INTENTION:_____

AFFIRMATION:_____

INTERPRETATION:_____

_____

REFLECTION: _____

DECK USED:

Monday the ___

1._____

_____

2._____

_____

3._____

_____

REFLECTION:_____

DECK USED:

Tuesday the ___

1._____

_____

2._____

_____

3._____

_____

REFLECTION:_____

DECK USED:

Wednesday the ___

1._____

_____

2._____

_____

3._____

_____

REFLECTION:_____

DECK USED:

Thursday the ___

1._____
_____
2._____
_____
3._____
_____
REFLECTION:_____
DECK USED:

Friday the ___

1._____
_____
2._____
_____
3._____
_____
REFLECTION:_____
DECK USED:

Saturday the ___

1._____
_____
2._____
_____
3._____
_____
REFLECTION:_____
DECK USED:

Sunday the ___

1._____
_____
2._____
_____
3._____
_____
REFLECTION:_____
DECK USED:

Week of: _____

INTENTION:_____

AFFIRMATION:_____

INTERPRETATION:_____

_____

REFLECTION: _____

DECK USED:

Monday the ___

1._____

_____

2._____

_____

3._____

_____

REFLECTION:_____

DECK USED:

Tuesday the ___

1._____

_____

2._____

_____

3._____

_____

REFLECTION:_____

DECK USED:

Wednesday the ___

1._____

_____

2._____

_____

3._____

_____

REFLECTION:_____

DECK USED:

Thursday the ___

1._____
_____
2._____
_____
3._____
_____

REFLECTION:_____

DECK USED:

Friday the ___

1._____
_____
2._____
_____
3._____
_____

REFLECTION:_____

DECK USED:

Saturday the ___

1._____
_____
2._____
_____
3._____
_____

REFLECTION:_____

DECK USED:

Sunday the ___

1._____
_____
2._____
_____
3._____
_____

REFLECTION:_____

DECK USED:

Week of: _____

INTENTION:_____

AFFIRMATION:_____

INTERPRETATION:_____

_____

REFLECTION: _____

DECK USED:

Monday the ___

1._____

_____

2._____

_____

3._____

_____

REFLECTION:_____

DECK USED:

Tuesday the ___

1._____

_____

2._____

_____

3._____

_____

REFLECTION:_____

DECK USED:

Wednesday the ___

1._____

_____

2._____

_____

3._____

_____

REFLECTION:_____

DECK USED:

Thursday the _ _ _

1._____
_____

2._____
_____

3._____
_____

REFLECTION:_____

DECK USED:

Friday the _ _ _

1._____
_____

2._____
_____

3._____
_____

REFLECTION:_____

DECK USED:

Saturday the _ _ _

1._____
_____

2._____
_____

3._____
_____

REFLECTION:_____

DECK USED:

Sunday the _ _ _

1._____
_____

2._____
_____

3._____
_____

REFLECTION:_____

DECK USED:

Week of: _____

INTENTION:_____

AFFIRMATION:_____

INTERPRETATION:_____

_____

REFLECTION: _____

DECK USED:

Monday the ___

1._____

_____

2._____

_____

3._____

_____

REFLECTION:_____

DECK USED:

Tuesday the ___

1._____

_____

2._____

_____

3._____

_____

REFLECTION:_____

DECK USED:

Wednesday the ___

1._____

_____

2._____

_____

3._____

_____

REFLECTION:_____

DECK USED:

Thursday the ___

1._____
_____
2._____
_____
3._____
_____
REFLECTION:_____
DECK USED:

Friday the ___

1._____
_____
2._____
_____
3._____
_____
REFLECTION:_____
DECK USED:

Saturday the ___

1._____
_____
2._____
_____
3._____
_____
REFLECTION:_____
DECK USED:

Sunday the ___

1._____
_____
2._____
_____
3._____
_____
REFLECTION:_____
DECK USED:

MONTH:_____ FULL MOON: _____ NEW MOON:_____

Sunday	Monday	Tuesday	Wednesday	Thursday	Friday	Saturday

September

MONTHLY ENERGY

DECK USED:_____

New moon
_____
_____

Full moon
_____
_____

LOVE

MONEY

WORK

HEALTH

SPIRIT

MONTHLY ENERGY:_____
_____
_____

LOVE: _____
_____
_____

MONEY: _____
_____
_____

WORK: _____
_____
_____

HEALTH: _____
_____
_____

SPIRIT:_____
_____
_____

END OF THE MONTH REFLECTION: _____
_____
_____
_____
_____
_____
_____

New Moon Spread

THIS TIME IS ABOUT NEW BEGINNINGS, PLANTING SEEDS, AND SETTING YOUR INTENTIONS FOR THE LUNAR CYCLE.

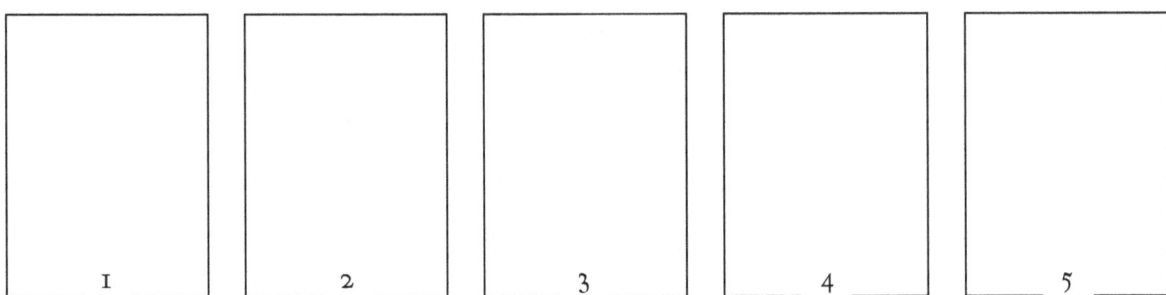

THIS IS A TIME TO MANIFEST YOUR DREAMS!

1. Your energy this month
2. A new opportunity
3. How to make things happen
4. Where I need to grow
5. Guidance from my guides

REFLECTIONS:_____
_____
_____
_____
_____
_____
_____
_____
_____
_____
_____

New Moon Intentions

MANIFEST YOUR DREAMS.

Full Moon Spread

THE FULL MOON IS THE CULMINATION OF OUR INTENTION. IT IS ABOUT ILLUMINATION AND LETTING GO OF WHAT IS NO LONGER NEEDED

My favorite spread for a full moon is a variation on what I do daily. I ask a single question, but I use 3 cards to answer it. I find that I get readings with lots of depth and details when I read this way.

RELEASE:
WHAT NO LONGER SERVES ME?

ILLUMINATION:
WHAT HIDDEN THINGS IS THE
MOON REVEALING TO ME?

TRANSFORMATION:
WHAT IS CHANGING?

REFLECTIONS:_____

_____

_____

_____

_____

_____

_____

_____

Full Moon Intentions

THIS IS A TIME TO CELEBRATE THE CULMINATION OF YOUR INTENTION.

Week of: _____

INTENTION:_____

AFFIRMATION:_____

INTERPRETATION:_____

_____

REFLECTION: _____

DECK USED:

Monday the ___

1._____

_____

2._____

_____

3._____

_____

REFLECTION:_____

DECK USED:

Tuesday the ___

1._____

_____

2._____

_____

3._____

_____

REFLECTION:_____

DECK USED:

Wednesday the ___

1._____

_____

2._____

_____

3._____

_____

REFLECTION:_____

DECK USED:

Thursday the ___

1._____
_____
2._____
_____
3._____
_____
REFLECTION:_____
DECK USED:

Friday the ___

1._____
_____
2._____
_____
3._____
_____
REFLECTION:_____
DECK USED:

Saturday the ___

1._____
_____
2._____
_____
3._____
_____
REFLECTION:_____
DECK USED:

Sunday the ___

1._____
_____
2._____
_____
3._____
_____
REFLECTION:_____
DECK USED:

Week of: _____

INTENTION:_____

AFFIRMATION:_____

INTERPRETATION:_____

_____

REFLECTION: _____

DECK USED:

Monday the ___

1._____

_____

2._____

_____

3._____

_____

REFLECTION:_____

DECK USED:

Tuesday the ___

1._____

_____

2._____

_____

3._____

_____

REFLECTION:_____

DECK USED:

Wednesday the ___

1._____

_____

2._____

_____

3._____

_____

REFLECTION:_____

DECK USED:

Thursday the ___

1._____
_____
2._____
_____
3._____
_____

REFLECTION:_____

DECK USED:

Friday the ___

1._____
_____
2._____
_____
3._____
_____

REFLECTION:_____

DECK USED:

Saturday the ___

1._____
_____
2._____
_____
3._____
_____

REFLECTION:_____

DECK USED:

Sunday the ___

1._____
_____
2._____
_____
3._____
_____

REFLECTION:_____

DECK USED:

Week of: _____

INTENTION:_____

AFFIRMATION:_____

INTERPRETATION:_____

_____

REFLECTION: _____

DECK USED:

Monday the ___

1._____

_____

2._____

_____

3._____

_____

REFLECTION:_____

DECK USED:

Tuesday the ___

1._____

_____

2._____

_____

3._____

_____

REFLECTION:_____

DECK USED:

Wednesday the ___

1._____

_____

2._____

_____

3._____

_____

REFLECTION:_____

DECK USED:

Thursday the ___

1._____
_____
2._____
_____
3._____
_____

REFLECTION:_____

DECK USED:

Friday the ___

1._____
_____
2._____
_____
3._____
_____

REFLECTION:_____

DECK USED:

Saturday the ___

1._____
_____
2._____
_____
3._____
_____

REFLECTION:_____

DECK USED:

Sunday the ___

1._____
_____
2._____
_____
3._____
_____

REFLECTION:_____

DECK USED:

Week of: _____

INTENTION:_____

AFFIRMATION:_____

INTERPRETATION:_____
_____

REFLECTION: _____

DECK USED:

Monday the ___

1._____
_____
2._____
_____
3._____
_____

REFLECTION:_____

DECK USED:

Tuesday the ___

1._____
_____
2._____
_____
3._____
_____

REFLECTION:_____

DECK USED:

Wednesday the ___

1._____
_____
2._____
_____
3._____
_____

REFLECTION:_____

DECK USED:

Thursday the ___

1._____

_____

2._____

_____

3._____

_____

REFLECTION:_____

DECK USED:

Friday the ___

1._____

_____

2._____

_____

3._____

_____

REFLECTION:_____

DECK USED:

Saturday the ___

1._____

_____

2._____

_____

3._____

_____

REFLECTION:_____

DECK USED:

Sunday the ___

1._____

_____

2._____

_____

3._____

_____

REFLECTION:_____

DECK USED:

Week of: _____

INTENTION:_____

AFFIRMATION:_____

INTERPRETATION:_____

_____

REFLECTION: _____

DECK USED:

Monday the ___

1._____

_____

2._____

_____

3._____

_____

REFLECTION:_____

DECK USED:

Tuesday the ___

1._____

_____

2._____

_____

3._____

_____

REFLECTION:_____

DECK USED:

Wednesday the ___

1._____

_____

2._____

_____

3._____

_____

REFLECTION:_____

DECK USED:

Thursday the ___

1._____
_____

2._____
_____

3._____
_____

REFLECTION:_____

DECK USED:

Friday the ___

1._____
_____

2._____
_____

3._____
_____

REFLECTION:_____

DECK USED:

Saturday the ___

1._____
_____

2._____
_____

3._____
_____

REFLECTION:_____

DECK USED:

Sunday the ___

1._____
_____

2._____
_____

3._____
_____

REFLECTION:_____

DECK USED:

MONTH:_____ FULL MOON: _____ NEW MOON:_____

Sunday	Monday	Tuesday	Wednesday	Thursday	Friday	Saturday

October

MONTHLY
ENERGY

DECK USED:_____

⬤ NEW MOON
_____
_____

◐ FULL MOON
_____
_____

LOVE   MONEY   WORK   HEALTH   SPIRIT

MONTHLY ENERGY:_____
_____
_____

LOVE: _____
_____
_____

MONEY: _____
_____
_____

WORK: _____
_____
_____

HEALTH: _____
_____
_____

SPIRIT:_____
_____
_____

END OF THE MONTH REFLECTION: _____
_____
_____
_____
_____
_____
_____

New Moon Spread

THIS TIME IS ABOUT NEW BEGINNINGS, PLANTING SEEDS, AND SETTING YOUR INTENTIONS FOR THE LUNAR CYCLE.

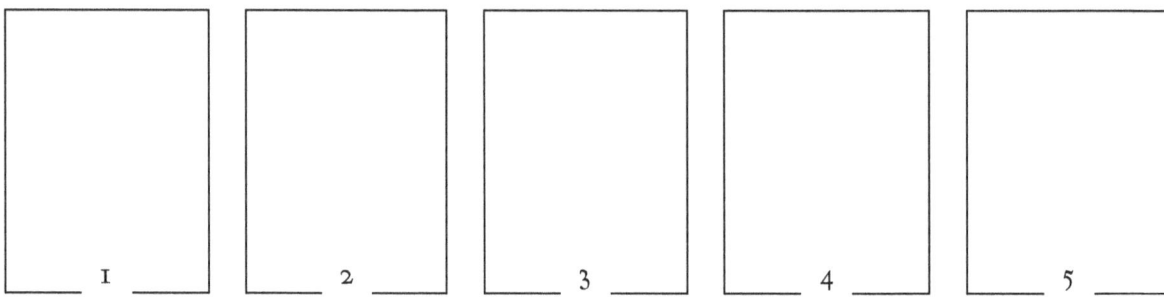

1 2 3 4 5

THIS IS A TIME TO MANIFEST YOUR DREAMS!

1. Your energy this month
2. A new opportunity
3. How to make things happen
4. Where I need to grow
5. Guidance from my guides

REFLECTIONS:_____

_____

_____

_____

_____

_____

_____

_____

_____

_____

_____

New Moon Intentions

MANIFEST YOUR DREAMS.

Full Moon Spread

THE FULL MOON IS THE CULMINATION OF OUR INTENTION.
IT IS ABOUT ILLUMINATION AND LETTING GO OF WHAT IS NO LONGER NEEDED

My favorite spread for a full moon is a variation on what I do daily. I ask a single question, but I use 3 cards to answer it. I find that I get readings with lots of depth and details when I read this way.

RELEASE:
WHAT NO LONGER SERVES ME?

ILLUMINATION:
WHAT HIDDEN THINGS IS THE
MOON REVEALING TO ME?

TRANSFORMATION:
WHAT IS CHANGING?

REFLECTIONS:_____

_____

_____

_____

_____

_____

_____

_____

Full Moon Intentions

THIS IS A TIME TO CELEBRATE THE CULMINATION OF YOUR INTENTION.

Week of: _____

INTENTION:_____

AFFIRMATION:_____

INTERPRETATION:_____

_____

REFLECTION: _____

DECK USED:

Monday the ___

1._____

_____

2._____

_____

3._____

_____

REFLECTION:_____

DECK USED:

Tuesday the ___

1._____

_____

2._____

_____

3._____

_____

REFLECTION:_____

DECK USED:

Wednesday the ___

1._____

_____

2._____

_____

3._____

_____

REFLECTION:_____

DECK USED:

Thursday the ___

1._____
_____
2._____
_____
3._____
_____

REFLECTION:_____

DECK USED:

Friday the ___

1._____
_____
2._____
_____
3._____
_____

REFLECTION:_____

DECK USED:

Saturday the ___

1._____
_____
2._____
_____
3._____
_____

REFLECTION:_____

DECK USED:

Sunday the ___

1._____
_____
2._____
_____
3._____
_____

REFLECTION:_____

DECK USED:

Week of: _____

INTENTION:_____

AFFIRMATION:_____

INTERPRETATION:_____

_____

REFLECTION: _____

DECK USED:

Monday the ___

1._____

_____

2._____

_____

3._____

_____

REFLECTION:_____

DECK USED:

Tuesday the ___

1._____

_____

2._____

_____

3._____

_____

REFLECTION:_____

DECK USED:

Wednesday the ___

1._____

_____

2._____

_____

3._____

_____

REFLECTION:_____

DECK USED:

Thursday the ___

1._____
_____
2._____
_____
3._____
_____

REFLECTION:_____

DECK USED:

Friday the ___

1._____
_____
2._____
_____
3._____
_____

REFLECTION:_____

DECK USED:

Saturday the ___

1._____
_____
2._____
_____
3._____
_____

REFLECTION:_____

DECK USED:

Sunday the ___

1._____
_____
2._____
_____
3._____
_____

REFLECTION:_____

DECK USED:

Week of: _____

INTENTION:_____

AFFIRMATION:_____

INTERPRETATION:_____

_____

REFLECTION: _____

DECK USED:

Monday the ___

1._____

_____

2._____

_____

3._____

_____

REFLECTION:_____

DECK USED:

Tuesday the ___

1._____

_____

2._____

_____

3._____

_____

REFLECTION:_____

DECK USED:

Wednesday the ___

1._____

_____

2._____

_____

3._____

_____

REFLECTION:_____

DECK USED:

Thursday the ___

1._____

_____

2._____

_____

3._____

_____

REFLECTION:_____

DECK USED:

Friday the ___

1._____

_____

2._____

_____

3._____

_____

REFLECTION:_____

DECK USED:

Saturday the ___

1._____

_____

2._____

_____

3._____

_____

REFLECTION:_____

DECK USED:

Sunday the ___

1._____

_____

2._____

_____

3._____

_____

REFLECTION:_____

DECK USED:

Week of: _____

INTENTION:_____

AFFIRMATION:_____

INTERPRETATION:_____

_____

REFLECTION: _____

DECK USED:

Monday the ___

1._____

_____

2._____

_____

3._____

_____

REFLECTION:_____

DECK USED:

Tuesday the ___

1._____

_____

2._____

_____

3._____

_____

REFLECTION:_____

DECK USED:

Wednesday the ___

1._____

_____

2._____

_____

3._____

_____

REFLECTION:_____

DECK USED:

Thursday the ___

1._____
_____
2._____
_____
3._____
_____

REFLECTION:_____

DECK USED:

Friday the ___

1._____
_____
2._____
_____
3._____
_____

REFLECTION:_____

DECK USED:

Saturday the ___

1._____
_____
2._____
_____
3._____
_____

REFLECTION:_____

DECK USED:

Sunday the ___

1._____
_____
2._____
_____
3._____
_____

REFLECTION:_____

DECK USED:

Week of: _____

INTENTION:_____

AFFIRMATION:_____

INTERPRETATION:_____

_____

REFLECTION: _____

DECK USED:

Monday the _ _ _

1._____

_____

2._____

_____

3._____

_____

REFLECTION:_____

DECK USED:

Tuesday the _ _ _

1._____

_____

2._____

_____

3._____

_____

REFLECTION:_____

DECK USED:

Wednesday the _ _ _

1._____

_____

2._____

_____

3._____

_____

REFLECTION:_____

DECK USED:

Thursday the ___

1._____
_____

2._____
_____

3._____
_____

REFLECTION:_____

DECK USED:

Friday the ___

1._____
_____

2._____
_____

3._____
_____

REFLECTION:_____

DECK USED:

Saturday the ___

1._____
_____

2._____
_____

3._____
_____

REFLECTION:_____

DECK USED:

Sunday the ___

1._____
_____

2._____
_____

3._____
_____

REFLECTION:_____

DECK USED:

MONTH:_____ FULL MOON: _____ NEW MOON:_____

Sunday	Monday	Tuesday	Wednesday	Thursday	Friday	Saturday

November

Monthly
Energy

Deck used:_____

New moon
_____
_____

Full moon
_____
_____

Love

Money

Work

Health

Spirit

Monthly Energy:_____
_____
_____

Love: _____
_____
_____

Money: _____
_____
_____

Work: _____
_____
_____

Health: _____
_____
_____

Spirit:_____
_____
_____

End of the Month Reflection: _____
_____
_____
_____
_____
_____
_____

New Moon Spread

THIS TIME IS ABOUT NEW BEGINNINGS, PLANTING SEEDS, AND SETTING YOUR INTENTIONS FOR THE LUNAR CYCLE.

1	2	3	4	5

THIS IS A TIME TO MANIFEST YOUR DREAMS!

1. Your energy this month
2. A new opportunity
3. How to make things happen
4. Where I need to grow
5. Guidance from my guides

REFLECTIONS:_____

_____

_____

_____

_____

_____

_____

_____

_____

_____

_____

_____

New Moon Intentions

MANIFEST YOUR DREAMS.

Full Moon Spread

THE FULL MOON IS THE CULMINATION OF OUR INTENTION. IT IS ABOUT ILLUMINATION AND LETTING GO OF WHAT IS NO LONGER NEEDED

My favorite spread for a full moon is a variation on what I do daily. I ask a single question, but I use 3 cards to answer it. I find that I get readings with lots of depth and details when I read this way.

RELEASE:
WHAT NO LONGER SERVES ME?

ILLUMINATION:
WHAT HIDDEN THINGS IS THE
MOON REVEALING TO ME?

TRANSFORMATION:
WHAT IS CHANGING?

REFLECTIONS:_____
_____
_____
_____
_____
_____
_____
_____

Full Moon Intentions

THIS IS A TIME TO CELEBRATE THE CULMINATION OF YOUR INTENTION.

Week of: _____

INTENTION:_____

AFFIRMATION:_____

INTERPRETATION:_____

_____

REFLECTION: _____

DECK USED:

Monday the ___

1._____

_____

2._____

_____

3._____

_____

REFLECTION:_____

DECK USED:

Tuesday the ___

1._____

_____

2._____

_____

3._____

_____

REFLECTION:_____

DECK USED:

Wednesday the ___

1._____

_____

2._____

_____

3._____

_____

REFLECTION:_____

DECK USED:

Thursday the ___

1._____
_____
2._____
_____
3._____
_____

REFLECTION:_____

DECK USED:

Friday the ___

1._____
_____
2._____
_____
3._____
_____

REFLECTION:_____

DECK USED:

Saturday the ___

1._____
_____
2._____
_____
3._____
_____

REFLECTION:_____

DECK USED:

Sunday the ___

1._____
_____
2._____
_____
3._____
_____

REFLECTION:_____

DECK USED:

Week of: _____

INTENTION:_____

AFFIRMATION:_____

INTERPRETATION:_____

_____

REFLECTION: _____

DECK USED:

Monday the ___

1._____

_____

2._____

_____

3._____

_____

REFLECTION:_____

DECK USED:

Tuesday the ___

1._____

_____

2._____

_____

3._____

_____

REFLECTION:_____

DECK USED:

Wednesday the ___

1._____

_____

2._____

_____

3._____

_____

REFLECTION:_____

DECK USED:

Thursday the ___

1._____
_____
2._____
_____
3._____
_____

REFLECTION:_____

DECK USED:

Friday the ___

1._____
_____
2._____
_____
3._____
_____

REFLECTION:_____

DECK USED:

Saturday the ___

1._____
_____
2._____
_____
3._____
_____

REFLECTION:_____

DECK USED:

Sunday the ___

1._____
_____
2._____
_____
3._____
_____

REFLECTION:_____

DECK USED:

Week of: _____

INTENTION:_____

AFFIRMATION:_____

INTERPRETATION:_____

_____

REFLECTION: _____

DECK USED:

Monday the ___

1._____

_____

2._____

_____

3._____

_____

REFLECTION:_____

DECK USED:

Tuesday the ___

1._____

_____

2._____

_____

3._____

_____

REFLECTION:_____

DECK USED:

Wednesday the ___

1._____

_____

2._____

_____

3._____

_____

REFLECTION:_____

DECK USED:

Thursday the ___

1._____
_____
2._____
_____
3._____
_____

REFLECTION:_____

DECK USED:

Friday the ___

1._____
_____
2._____
_____
3._____
_____

REFLECTION:_____

DECK USED:

Saturday the ___

1._____
_____
2._____
_____
3._____
_____

REFLECTION:_____

DECK USED:

Sunday the ___

1._____
_____
2._____
_____
3._____
_____

REFLECTION:_____

DECK USED:

Week of: _____

INTENTION:_____

AFFIRMATION:_____

INTERPRETATION:_____

_____

REFLECTION: _____

DECK USED:

Monday the ___

1._____

_____

2._____

_____

3._____

_____

REFLECTION:_____

DECK USED:

Tuesday the ___

1._____

_____

2._____

_____

3._____

_____

REFLECTION:_____

DECK USED:

Wednesday the ___

1._____

_____

2._____

_____

3._____

_____

REFLECTION:_____

DECK USED:

Thursday the ___

1._____
_____
2._____
_____
3._____
_____

REFLECTION:_____

DECK USED:

Friday the ___

1._____
_____
2._____
_____
3._____
_____

REFLECTION:_____

DECK USED:

Saturday the ___

1._____
_____
2._____
_____
3._____
_____

REFLECTION:_____

DECK USED:

Sunday the ___

1._____
_____
2._____
_____
3._____
_____

REFLECTION:_____

DECK USED:

Week of: _____

INTENTION:_____

AFFIRMATION:_____

INTERPRETATION:_____

_____

REFLECTION: _____

DECK USED:

Monday the ___

1._____

_____

2._____

_____

3._____

_____

REFLECTION:_____

DECK USED:

Tuesday the ___

1._____

_____

2._____

_____

3._____

_____

REFLECTION:_____

DECK USED:

Wednesday the ___

1._____

_____

2._____

_____

3._____

_____

REFLECTION:_____

DECK USED:

Thursday the ___

1._____
_____

2._____
_____

3._____
_____

REFLECTION:_____

DECK USED:

Friday the ___

1._____
_____

2._____
_____

3._____
_____

REFLECTION:_____

DECK USED:

Saturday the ___

1._____
_____

2._____
_____

3._____
_____

REFLECTION:_____

DECK USED:

Sunday the ___

1._____
_____

2._____
_____

3._____
_____

REFLECTION:_____

DECK USED:

MONTH:_____ FULL MOON: _____ NEW MOON:_____						
Sunday	Monday	Tuesday	Wednesday	Thursday	Friday	Saturday

December

MONTHLY ENERGY

DECK USED:_____

NEW MOON
_____
_____

FULL MOON
_____
_____

LOVE   MONEY   WORK   HEALTH   SPIRIT

MONTHLY ENERGY:_____
_____
_____

LOVE: _____
_____
_____

MONEY: _____
_____
_____

WORK: _____
_____
_____

HEALTH: _____
_____
_____

SPIRIT:_____
_____
_____

END OF THE MONTH REFLECTION: _____
_____
_____
_____
_____
_____
_____

New Moon Spread

THIS TIME IS ABOUT NEW BEGINNINGS, PLANTING SEEDS, AND SETTING YOUR INTENTIONS FOR THE LUNAR CYCLE.

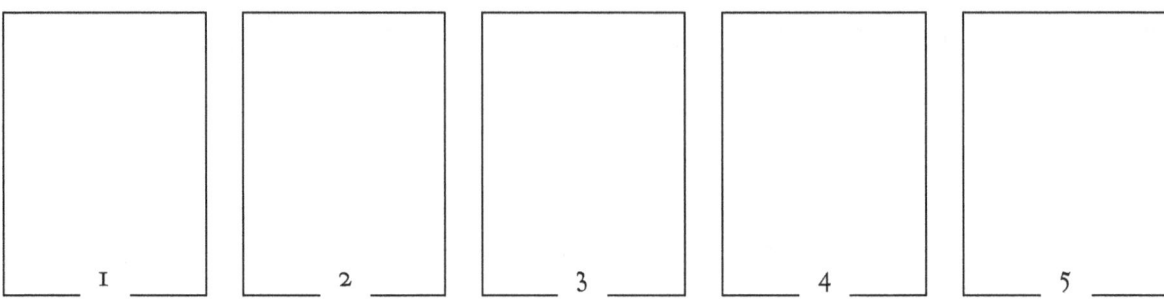

THIS IS A TIME TO MANIFEST YOUR DREAMS!

1.   Your energy this month
2.   A new opportunity
3.   How to make things happen
4.   Where I need to grow
5.   Guidance from my guides

REFLECTIONS:_____

_____

_____

_____

_____

_____

_____

_____

_____

_____

_____

_____

New Moon Intentions

MANIFEST YOUR DREAMS.

Full Moon Spread

THE FULL MOON IS THE CULMINATION OF OUR INTENTION. IT IS ABOUT ILLUMINATION AND LETTING GO OF WHAT IS NO LONGER NEEDED

My favorite spread for a full moon is a variation on what I do daily. I ask a single question, but I use 3 cards to answer it. I find that I get readings with lots of depth and details when I read this way.

RELEASE:
WHAT NO LONGER SERVES ME?

ILLUMINATION:
WHAT HIDDEN THINGS IS THE
MOON REVEALING TO ME?

TRANSFORMATION:
WHAT IS CHANGING?

REFLECTIONS:_____
_____
_____
_____
_____
_____
_____
_____

Full Moon Intentions

THIS IS A TIME TO CELEBRATE THE CULMINATION OF YOUR INTENTION.

Week of: _____

INTENTION:_____

AFFIRMATION:_____

INTERPRETATION:_____

_____

REFLECTION: _____

DECK USED:

Monday the ___

1._____

_____

2._____

_____

3._____

_____

REFLECTION:_____

DECK USED:

Tuesday the ___

1._____

_____

2._____

_____

3._____

_____

REFLECTION:_____

DECK USED:

Wednesday the ___

1._____

_____

2._____

_____

3._____

_____

REFLECTION:_____

DECK USED:

Thursday the ___

1._____
_____
2._____
_____
3._____
_____

REFLECTION:_____

DECK USED:

Friday the ___

1._____
_____
2._____
_____
3._____
_____

REFLECTION:_____

DECK USED:

Saturday the ___

1._____
_____
2._____
_____
3._____
_____

REFLECTION:_____

DECK USED:

Sunday the ___

1._____
_____
2._____
_____
3._____
_____

REFLECTION:_____

DECK USED:

Week of: _____

INTENTION:_____

AFFIRMATION:_____

INTERPRETATION:_____

_____

REFLECTION: _____

DECK USED:

Monday the ___

1._____

_____

2._____

_____

3._____

_____

REFLECTION:_____

DECK USED:

Tuesday the ___

1._____

_____

2._____

_____

3._____

_____

REFLECTION:_____

DECK USED:

Wednesday the ___

1._____

_____

2._____

_____

3._____

_____

REFLECTION:_____

DECK USED:

Thursday the ___

1._____

_____

2._____

_____

3._____

_____

REFLECTION:_____

DECK USED:

Friday the ___

1._____

_____

2._____

_____

3._____

_____

REFLECTION:_____

DECK USED:

Saturday the ___

1._____

_____

2._____

_____

3._____

_____

REFLECTION:_____

DECK USED:

Sunday the ___

1._____

_____

2._____

_____

3._____

_____

REFLECTION:_____

DECK USED:

Week of: _____

INTENTION:_____

AFFIRMATION:_____

INTERPRETATION:_____

_____

REFLECTION: _____

DECK USED:

Monday the ___

1._____

_____

2._____

_____

3._____

_____

REFLECTION:_____

DECK USED:

Tuesday the ___

1._____

_____

2._____

_____

3._____

_____

REFLECTION:_____

DECK USED:

Wednesday the ___

1._____

_____

2._____

_____

3._____

_____

REFLECTION:_____

DECK USED:

Thursday the ___

1._____
_____
2._____
_____
3._____
_____
REFLECTION:_____
DECK USED:

Friday the ___

1._____
_____
2._____
_____
3._____
_____
REFLECTION:_____
DECK USED:

Saturday the ___

1._____
_____
2._____
_____
3._____
_____
REFLECTION:_____
DECK USED:

Sunday the ___

1._____
_____
2._____
_____
3._____
_____
REFLECTION:_____
DECK USED:

Week of: _____

INTENTION:_____

AFFIRMATION:_____

INTERPRETATION:_____

_____

REFLECTION: _____

DECK USED:

Monday the ___

1._____

_____

2._____

_____

3._____

_____

REFLECTION:_____

DECK USED:

Tuesday the ___

1._____

_____

2._____

_____

3._____

_____

REFLECTION:_____

DECK USED:

Wednesday the ___

1._____

_____

2._____

_____

3._____

_____

REFLECTION:_____

DECK USED:

Thursday the ___

1._____

_____

2._____

_____

3._____

_____

REFLECTION:_____

DECK USED:

Friday the ___

1._____

_____

2._____

_____

3._____

_____

REFLECTION:_____

DECK USED:

Saturday the ___

1._____

_____

2._____

_____

3._____

_____

REFLECTION:_____

DECK USED:

Sunday the ___

1._____

_____

2._____

_____

3._____

_____

REFLECTION:_____

DECK USED:

	Week of: _____
	INTENTION:_____
	AFFIRMATION:_____

INTERPRETATION:_____
_____
REFLECTION: _____
DECK USED:

Monday the ___

1._____
_____
2._____
_____
3._____
_____
REFLECTION:_____
DECK USED:

Tuesday the ___

1._____
_____
2._____
_____
3._____
_____
REFLECTION:_____
DECK USED:

Wednesday the ___

1._____
_____
2._____
_____
3._____
_____
REFLECTION:_____
DECK USED:

Thursday the ___

1. _____

_____

2. _____

_____

3. _____

_____

REFLECTION: _____

DECK USED:

Friday the ___

1. _____

_____

2. _____

_____

3. _____

_____

REFLECTION: _____

DECK USED:

Saturday the ___

1. _____

_____

2. _____

_____

3. _____

_____

REFLECTION: _____

DECK USED:

Sunday the ___

1. _____

_____

2. _____

_____

3. _____

_____

REFLECTION: _____

DECK USED: